Dedicated to the indefatigable Morag Prunty
for her belief and determination the Home Place find a new
readership

I myself do not approve of my own nostalgia for a way of life that was so hard on men, women and children and that led to so much self-destructiveness. Maybe it will be a healthier Ireland when it is, effectively, a series of housing estates interspersed with towns. The feel of a landscape, however, shaped to a communal purpose by long experience, will be gone.

Nuala O Faolain
Irish Times Magazine
17th February 2001.

It is the chilling nature of modern society to find an ignorance of geography, local or national, as excusable as an ignorance of hand tools; and to find the commitment of people to their home places only momentarily entertaining. And finally naïve.

Barry Lopez
About This Life
The Harvill Press, 1999.

CONTENTS

FOREWORD

Along with a new chapter to end this reissue of The Home Place, I wanted to return to the National Geographic journal mentioned at the start. In the November edition from 1978, a two-page spread of photographs taken by Adam Woolfitt documented my mother and father at work on their small farm in Crosshill in the North West of Ireland. Ever since, images from the assignment keep cropping up in unforeseen places, trailing a kite-tail of free floating stories, starting when The Home Place was first published.

I was a guest on the RTE daytime television programme Open House where I met the producer Larry Masterson. He looked at the copy of the National Geographic I'd brought along and told me that early on in Martin Scorsese's Goodfellas there's a scene where on his way to dispose of a body, the character played by Joe Pesci stops at his mother's house. She is a Sunday painter and she shows him and his friends, played by Robert De Niro and Ray Liotta, her latest work of a man seated in a boat with two dogs. The man is John Weaving, a river-nomad photographed with his dogs, Brocky and Twiggy, in the same article in which my parents appeared.

It's worth adding that John Weaving took up as a navigational consultant and oddjobber after he quit a career in banking to live on a 60-foot barge on the River Shannon. He also waged a far-sighted campaign against the low modern bridges being built to span the river and its waterways, believing – as happened in the 1990s – that the Shannon-Erne Waterway would one day reopen and clearance would be needed for family size pleasure craft.

The article in the Geographic was called 'Where the River Shannon Flows'. It was written by the assistant editor at the time, Allan C. Fisher, Jr, and the title comes from a James Russell song composed in 1904. It's a sweet song that has been covered over the years by John McCormack and Bridie Gallagher. The original James Russell version was intended to brighten up 'The Irish Servant Girls' sketch that he, and his brother John, had staged in the theatres of New York since the late 1870s. This was a knockabout routine in which the vaudeville performers dressed up as housemaids in skirts and long white aprons, and James added a red wig and covered his dress with green ribbons. Between songs the brothers hit each other with broomsticks, winked at men in the audience, and exposed their underwear.

In late January 1907, the Russell brothers were scheduled to perform in the Victoria Theatre in New York City. The moment they appeared on stage, a hundred-strong group of protestors belonging to the newly formed 'Society for the Prevention of Ridiculous and Pervasive Misrepresentation of the Irish Character' roared that they should be taken off. As the catcalls subsided Thomas P. Tuite, an Irish-American war veteran, warned that if they didn't stop the show, 'clean, manly men' would stop them.

The brothers took flight, but renamed the show 'The Stage Struck Maid', and playing down the camp, they tried staging a tamer version in the Orpheum Theatre in Brooklyn. Here they were pelted with eggs and lemons to the point where they were reported to resemble 'egg and lemon soufflé'. And by 1913 the curtain had not only come down on the show, but on the Russell brother's careers, although you can still enjoy vintage recordings of "Where the River Shannon Flows".

On September 11, 2005, the Sunday Times Culture Magazine carried a piece on John McGahern's Memoir. Along with the John Carey review there was a photograph captioned "County Leitrim where the author grew up".

In fact, it was another Adam Woollfitt photograph of the home place in Country Roscommon where I grew up. Taken at the same time as the National Geographic shots, the fine print at the side credited the Corbis agency for its use. It should have dawned on me sooner that along with what's available through Corbis, the photographer has his own dedicated website with a vast back catalogue of his work including other unused photos from the Geographic assignment.

So I was more charmed than surprised when looking through The Irish Heritage Cookbook by Biddy White Lennon and Georgina Campbell, I spotted in the lower corner of page 15 another Adam Woolfitt shot I hadn't seen before of my father seated with his back to the camera on a lead-painted orange coloured cart hauling a can of milk intended for the co-operative creamery in Kiltoghert, a location that certainly fitted the setting for the late John McGahern short story, 'The Creamery Manager'.

I was taken unawares, however, when Stella Mew, the President of the Yeats Society in Sligo, handed me a copy of a book called Turf Smoke published by the Sligo Active Retirement Association SARA. She was bringing it to my attention in my capacity then as the Writer-in-Residence with Sligo Libraries. She had no idea why the picture on the cover completely threw me. But there was my father again, large as life, his left hand in his pocket, his right hand holding the bridle and leading his donkey and cart towards the lens and posterity.

The original photo-essay in the Geographic documented my father and mother, Matt and Ann Leyden carrying the ten gallon creamery can to the cart. Next up, Matt is digging the potatoes seen piling up in a red bucket. The same plastic bucket appears in his hand in the third photograph where my mother has her fingers stuck in the mouth of a suck calf and a black plastic bucket in her other hand where only flying droplets of milk remain.

She wears her headscarf tied under her chin, and a blue nylon housecoat with the sleeves rolled up. That outfit is the chief reason why she was happy for these images to slip out of mind. In the accompanying text the more formal version of her name, Ann, is used. And if my mother had gotten her way, she would have been photographed with her hair done, wearing her best outfit, along with her dearly loved string of pearls.

Adam Woolfitt wanted authenticity, where my mother wanted to be seen in a better light in photographs circulated around the world. For me, however, it's a lovely photograph of both my parents, and a truthful depiction. Though what held my eye when I looked again at these images years after they were taken was the fourth, full-page picture.

We see my father settled on the donkey cart setting out for the creamery collection point. He has his arm around our dog Sally securely ensconced in his lap. The dented creamery can stands in the middle of the cart with one blue timber sideboard up as it rolls under the green canopy of a young elm tree in full leaf spanning the laneway.

My father died in November 1987. The donkey we called 'Jackie' is long since gone. Sally lived for seventeen years, seeing me and my school going brothers grow up and leave home. The co-operative creamery was taken over by a conglomerate, and the cart fell apart with age, as did the tackle and the creamery can. The spokes of the cartwheels ended up as dividers in a bed for home-grown herbs. And even the young tree got Dutch Elm disease and had to be cut down. Time obliterated practically everything recorded in that set of photographs except the stories behind them that in writing The Home Place I set out to preserve.

THE SITUATION

We did not see ourselves as a remarkable, far-flung or endangered people. Our way of life, our attitudes, our humour and engagement with our home place hardly deserved the attention of the National Geographic Society. But the *National Geographic Magazine* for November 1978 included an article, 'Where the River Shannon Flows'. A map on page 657 showed the Shannon River: the longest river in Ireland or Britain, and the symbolic divide between the remainder of Ireland and the true West. Adam Woolfitt, the assignment photographer, included a two-page photo essay that highlighted my mother and father, Ann and Matt Leyden, on their family farm in County Roscommon overlooking the Shannon. A caption quoted my father: "Don't stay too long in this country or it will capture you."

Soon after the Shannon River article appeared, the postman began to arrive at our house on the mountain with letters from all over the world. Many of the letters were addressed simply to: 'Matt and Ann Leyden, Overlooking Lough Allen, Ireland'. Inevitably, some wrote to say they shared the family name and wondered if they were related. But the owner of a cattle station in Australia, and a woman from Saskatchewan in Canada, wrote from opposite ends of the earth to say they felt their lives had a lot in common with Ann and Matt on their 23-acre small-holding in the Northwest of Ireland. Another woman sent an oil painting of my mother and father at work in their romantic rural situation. And several of the correspondents came especially to Ireland to visit our home place, hoping to find a world as wholesome and gentle as the one portrayed in the photographs.

As the years passed, the *National Geographic* with the piece about my mother and father faded from memory. But I was browsing one day in the Dandelion second-hand bookshop in Dublin when I spotted a stack of back issues of the magazine. I delved into the pile and found the copy I had in mind, Vol. 154, No. 5, close to the bottom of the stack.

Seeing the photographs again provoked a complex mixture of emotions. They presented a quaint and even corny tableau. And yet, Adam Woolfitt invented or contrived nothing. He showed exactly how we lived then. And it struck me how our lives and Ireland as a country and a society had changed; how much was gone, was passing quickly or about to be lost forever.

*

Discovering that back issue of the *National Geographic* turned out to be more than providential. I had another plan in mind besides furnishing the bookcase at home with a chronicle of my mother and father's lives 25 years ago. My mother's birthday was coming up. She would be 70 years of age at the end of August 2001. Her sister would turn seventy the same day, as they were identical twins.

I couldn't treat my mother without including her twin sister. But my mother and her twin were not ostentatious women; their guiding motto in life being: "Don't make a fuss". They were at their best amongst people they knew. And I had in mind a moderately extended family party, intimate and personal to them.

Then something terrible and unforeseen happened that threatened even the most humble celebration.

My mother's proper name was Ann, but everyone called her Nan. Just as her twin sister, Elizabeth, was better known as Lil. My mother lived in a traditional two-storey farmhouse in the parish of Kilronan in County Roscommon. Lil lived only a short distance away in a two-storey farmhouse outside the village of Keadue, also in County Roscommon. Built from the one blueprint, the home place and Lil's house were the same. The identical twins lived in identical farmhouses on equally small farms. Both women had three children: Lil had two girls and a boy, Nan had three boys. Both twins had spent the greater part of their lives looking after elderly relations. Both were farmers. Both widows. Nan's husband, Matt Leyden, – my father – died on the 6th of November 1987. Lil's husband, John Beirne, died the following month on the last day of December. My mother's health was good. But Lil was admitted that July to the Regional Hospital in Galway suffering from severe back pains. Lil told Nan she reckoned she had osteoporosis. The consultant diagnosed cancer.

Lil was transferred to Saint Luke's Hospital in Dublin for radiation therapy. And I was on the way to collect my mother to take her to Saint Luke's to see her twin sister. Seated beside me in the car, my wife Carmel couldn't hide her feelings. Though she was silent, the upset showed clearly in her eyes. Turning the car off the mountain road at the big sycamore tree that marked the laneway to the home place I felt anxious, yet ready for whatever had to be faced.

I drove slowly down the lane that inclined towards the house, noticing my mother had the place looking well: the lane resurfaced, the hedges on either side trimmed, the lawn cut and her garden full of flowers in bloom. The hay in the field nearest the house had been saved earlier in the summer and a second crop of after grass grew green and strong in the morning sunshine. Behind the house the pasture fields dropped away steeply, giving a view of the Arigna River that looped along the floor of the valley before taking a straight course into Lough Allen, the first lake of the Shannon River. The lake that morning looked pale and the far mountain featureless in a benign haze.

As we approached the farmhouse I saw my mother crossing the lawn to close the door of the greenhouse. On her way back we met in the yard. Knowing the journey we had ahead of us, our welcomes were underplayed, though we did kiss each other on the cheek - a new thing for us.

Our purpose was to accommodate my mother, but she fretted that she was holding up Carmel and myself when she said she had one last to chore to do before we hit the road. She had to feed Bob, the sheepdog. At the mention of his name Bob's ears dropped and he began to whine, sensing our visit meant that my mother would be gone for the day or longer and he would have to make do with one big feed and sleep in the hayshed until she got back.

We made good time once we crossed the Shannon and decided to stop again near water for something to eat at Fury's on the banks of the Royal Canal. After the rest stop, Carmel took over the driving. When the flow of cars on the N4 clotted into city traffic I read directions from the street map. Finding Highfield Road, we soon spotted the gateway to Saint Luke's.

"We're here," I said as the car swung around by the front entrance of probably the best known cancer treatment hospital in the country.

My mother found it hard to look directly at the building. She sat in the back of the car anxiously twisting the strap of her handbag. "I'm out walking the fields since I heard the news," she said. "I knew it wasn't good when they sent Lil to Saint Luke's."

We parked the car and walked towards the front entrance. As we walked under the trees in the leaf-dappled light, a middle-aged couple came towards us, headed for their own car. From the way they walked I knew they had been given bad news. Heads bent close, they were talking realistically, arms linked, supporting each other. The portents were bad. But from beyond the trees we heard a bout of laughter: a solidarity of cancer patients sitting around a lawn table, scarves covering their chemotherapy-bare heads. The survivors relating their stories.

We got directions to the ward and found Lil resting. She had just returned from that day's radium treatment. Her face looked more lined and shrunken than my mother's. She wore no make-up, her hair lay in tangles and her nightdress looked askew, as if she had been caught unexpectedly in the rush from her home to the hospital with not enough time to get ready.

We smiled and greeted one another as if we were just meeting by chance. Lil had lost weight. And she said she had a painful abscess on her gum, which meant she couldn't wear her dentures, causing her cheeks to cave further in. But she was alert and talkative, and stirred slightly to demonstrate that she had lost the power in one leg.

"What happened at all?" she asked. "I was in great fettle a month ago."

"You were doing so well," my mother said.

"Now I'm afraid to move in case the bone goes in my back," Lil said.

"I'll talk to the doctor," I said.

While Carmel and my mother chatted to Lil, I stepped into the corridor to have a word with the nurses at their station. They kept looking at Lil and her visitor, wondering if they were seeing right. I explained that the woman in the bed and my mother were twin sisters. They were obviously fond of Lil and when they spotted the doctor on the corridor they beckoned him over to have a word with me. He stood over six feet tall and was called Doctor Short.

Doctor Short said the radium treatment was an emergency intervention for spinal compaction. Without this intervention Lil would lose the use of her legs. He did not think the cancer in her spine was related to the procedure Lil had three years ago for breast cancer, but that wasn't his area. He could not rule out the possibility that the breast cancer and the spine cancer were secondary to a primary tumour, perhaps in the bowel. But again, that was not his area and he had not seen the results of the tests.

"So what's the prognosis?"

"I don't have enough information," he said. "But I'm hoping to get Elizabeth back on her feet. That's what we're doing here. That's what the radium treatment is for."

"Roughly how long has she got?"

"I couldn't say."

Doctor Short would not commit himself, but he indicated that for Lil it was not *if* but *when* she would die from the cancer in her backbone.

"A year?" I asked.

"Less," he said. It was like a perverse auction where I wanted to pay more and he kept bringing down the bid.

"Six months?"

"A lot depends on the test results. You really should talk to her consultant."

When he said that I knew she had nearer to three months.

As the truth sunk in, I was amazed at how calmly I took the inescapable certainty of Lil's death. The setting helped. There was an air of tranquility pervading Saint Luke's that I had experienced in no other hospital: a soothing absence of the rush and overload of acute hospital environments. It was not just the sense of pain buffered and fear subdued by the expert deployment of narcotics, chemical therapy and focused blasts of radiation; there was a reassuring sense of know-how matched against a deadly but not impossible challenge. A feeling reinforced by the staff who pointed out that in Saint Luke's today their successes outnumbered their losses in the fight against cancer.

Only not in Lil's case. For Lil it was too late.

When I returned, Lil had settled back into a heap of pillows.

"I thought I might get away without this," she said peering up at me with quick, watchful eyes.

I saw fear in the corner of her eyes, as she surely saw the evasion in mine. But the three women listened while I explained to the best of my ability how the radiation treatment was intended to give Lil back the power in her legs.

"The doctor is confident he'll have you back on your feet," I said.

Lil nodded smartly and said: "I'm bucked."

"No you're not," my mother said. "You shouldn't be talking like that."

To spare our feelings, I suspect, Lil rallied and said to Carmel, "You got your hair done."

Carmel said she was amazed Lil noticed.

"We were going to be hairdressers, you know," my mother said as she fondly patted Lil's tangled hair. At the touch of her sister's hand Lil bowed her head. I knew then I was not going to tell my mother what the doctor said to me - that death was inexorably stalking her twin.

It was time to go. But we kept stalling and finding little things to do. Throughout their lives my mother and her sister had never been very far or very long apart. And at that moment I wanted to sweep Lil up in my arms and run with her through the nearest exit to a hiding place in some Godforsaken part of the country where she could crouch quieter than a mouse while death would search, yet fail to find her, and so move on, allowing her a reprieve. But all I could do was press Lil's hand and fumble a goodbye, while Carmel refilled Lil's glass of 7-Up and my mother asked if Lil had enough clean underwear and nightdresses to last until the next visit.

Lil told us to hurry up or we'd get stuck in the evening traffic.

Shortly after leaving the hospital we got wedged in the rush hour congestion. As we crawled homeward in the evening traffic, I remembered Carmel telling me that when she saw the lines of cars on her first visit to Dublin as a child, she thought they were all going to the one funeral. And I thought of what Lil said as we were fixing the pillows to ease the pressure on her backbone. "I'm like a glass woman," she said. "The smallest tap and I'll break."

A FRONTIER SETTLEMENT

BOILING HEADS

When the twins, Nan and Lil, turned 13 years old in 1944, their parents took them out of school. They were needed to work on the farm at home. What did they expect? Opportunities were scarce. There was a war on. Sacrifices had to be made.

It happened the twins had reached an awkward age at an awkward time. In the aftermath of a divisive civil war the Irish Free State stayed out of the Allied war against the Nazis. Political expediency required the fledgling State to isolate itself from the war in mainland Europe. Neutrality encouraged the population to unite as a nation: a single people in one place adhering to a righteous, dour but unifying Roman Catholic faith.

Fingers were unthinkingly dipped in the holy water font inside the front door of most households and on every visit to the chapel. Practically every household had a Rosary beads, a portrait of the Sacred Heart and a crucifix nailed to the wall. Holy statues were popular; Saint Martin and the Child of Prague. Nobody missed mass or being seen at mass. Abstinence and pious observance ruled country people's lives in a strict regime of fasting on holy days and Fridays without meat. Women sat on the left - and men on the right-hand side of the chapel. The same segregation applied in the schoolhouse and the dancehall. Virginity was esteemed and childbirth thought to sully even married women, who had to be 'churched' in a furtive ritual conducted between the priest and the woman as an act of compulsory cleansing before the mother of a new baby could again receive Holy Communion.

Only the exacting Easter ceremonies and Corpus Christi processions allowed passion and spectacle, with colourful makeshift altars erected in open doorways and rose petals scattered underfoot to purify the journey of the Sacred Host in a sunburst gold monstrance. Public parades enacted at the sombre tempo of prayer.

Shortages and restrictions caused by the war forced Irish people to buy native goods regardless of the quality. Patriotism meant you couldn't complain. And the soles of Irish-made shoes were as thin as the jokes the people cracked - like the man who stole a rope and skipped it to England. In this prevailing climate of poverty and pious nationalism, the transatlantic passenger ship, the mail boat, and the cattle boat were the most widely chosen means of escape from a low wage, stagnant economy where tuberculosis raged, where death and disfigurement from polio were widespread, and the infant mortality rate was too shocking to be officially registered.

Despite these harsh conditions, the times weren't entirely bleak. Power lines were starting to span the roadsides and fields. And in the flickering light of paraffin-oil lamps and candles guttering from the draft under the door, the campaign began to get connected to the rural electrification schemes. In the early days, people considered it a waste of money to 'get in the current'. And they were suspicious of the men who came to measure the size of your house to establish the ground rent. "The mice'll eat the wires coming into the house," Nan's mother fretted. "We'll all be burned alive in our beds." Even Nan's father, Henry Joe McDermot, a smart man in his own right, said: "The cattle in the fields will be electrocuted."

The men putting up the poles also had their own brand of misinformation. When Nan's parents finally agreed to get connected, the workmen erected a pole in the centre of the good meadow field.

Garbed with spiked metal climbing boots and balanced at the top of a pole oozing creosote, the linesman seemed a terrifying figure. But Nan approached him to complain. She told him he had the pole in the wrong place. Could he not put it in a corner of the field? He told her the pole couldn't be moved. The electricity would get blocked if the wires came in at the wrong angle as the current wouldn't travel around sharp corners.

Meanwhile a slope too steep would cause the electricity to flow past the house. So the electricity poles went up in the middle of the three best meadow fields.

Families used the current sparingly at first. A house at the other end of the valley received an electricity bill for one unit. An official came out to investigate. The woman of the house said the electricity gave a powerful light while she put oil in the Tilly lamp. At home, when Nan and Lil sat up reading their *Titbits* magazines, they were warned not to be burning light.

Lil was the quieter of the two twins. But Nan clashed frequently with her parents, especially her mother, a grimly old-fashioned woman who had worked for several years in America as a maidservant and came home as unenlightened as she left. Mary McDermot maintained subscriptions to *The African Mission*, *The Far East*, *The Messenger*, and other religious magazines, but superstition ruled her life. She believed in bad-minded neighbours who could put an evil eye on a fine animal to make it sick, or conjure blight on a healthy crop of potatoes. Shoes left on the table were a certain cause of death in the house.

On the Eve of the Feast of Saint Martin, the 11th of November, the twins' mother killed a hen and sprinkled the blood in the four corners of the house to protect the yield of eggs.

"You'll clean up that mess yourself," Nan said, a spirited teenager at this stage.

"It's for the Saint," her mother said.

"It looks more like Devil-worship to me."

The twins' older sister, Teresa, went to America after the war to work. Several times a year she sent home bundles of magazines for Nan and Lil to read. Throughout the 1950s, the rich and famous were photographed in Sybil Connolly's Dublin salon wearing exclusive ball gowns, pleated linen creations and other eye-catching eveningwear. Country girls couldn't afford such high style, but the paper patterns that came in the post were starting to set home sewing machines singing. And what did every woman with a new dress want but a new hairdo.

Their mother and father said no. To become hairdressers Nan and Lil would have to serve an apprenticeship. Their sister, Teresa, had trained in the post office in Ballyfarnon. The experience became her passport to a job with the postal service in America. But until she qualified,

Teresa remained at the mercy of her employers, and paid them for the privilege.

The twins' mother always twisted her hair and pinned it at the back of her head into a bun, or what she called 'a poll'. She had no use for hot rollers and ammonia-strong setting lotions.

"Boiling heads." She dismissed the idea.

Lil backed down, ready to bide her time. But Nan was more impulsive and asked if she could do a correspondence course through a fashion academy. They would teach her how to design, cut and sew patterns using home assignments until she qualified as a dressmaker.

"Mantey making." Her mother belittled the notion and repeated for the twins what she told them before, "You're leaving school for good."

ARIGNA

On our way home from Saint Luke's Hospital we learned there had been an accident in the village. A lorry loaded with gravel took off on Chapel Hill, ploughed through the lower end of the cemetery wall, and smashed into the rear of the church in Arigna.

We detoured to have a look, taking the top road and then turning down Chapel Hill, a shortcut from Derrinavoggy Mountain into the valley. At the top of Chapel Hill stood a reservoir that supplied the village with poor quality water tainted with a rust-coloured scum we described as *reoite*. Below the reservoir on a steep slope lay the graveyard with a view of the valley and Lough Allen in the distance. On the far side of the lake stood Sliabh Anierinn and the Shannon Pot: the source of the Shannon River.

As children we called this graveyard in the middle of the valley 'the dead centre of Arigna'. At its foot stood the church. Then a scatter of dwelling houses, the parish hall, industrial buildings, coal yards, two shops, a post office and a pub.

At the church twin skid marks were scorched straight across a sharp bend and dip in the road, and a gap broken in the cemetery wall. The lorry rested at the bottom of the incline, the cab smashed, the front axle twisted and the driver's door hanging open. Despite the drop, the 20-ton lorry had not broken through when it hit the end wall of the chapel. But the overhead window was smashed and knocked out of its frame. Loose gravel had spilled from the back into the driver's cab and around the chapel yard. Normally, I wouldn't rubberneck around the scene of an accident, taking a ghoulish interest in the wreckage. But it was an unusual sight to see a 20-ton lorry – an emblem of the coal-mining village – crashed into the back of Arigna chapel.

Years before, it was an accident with a lorry that brought my father to the village of Arigna. At that time he was a young man from 'The Walk' on the outskirts of the town of Roscommon. He had a job looking after the grounds and stoking the boiler that heated the General Hospital. He worked alongside his sister's husband, Packie Sheerin, a jolly, outgoing man who also acted as a caddy for the doctors in the hospital. Packie happened to be away on the golf course the day the coal lorry from Arigna arrived. It was left to Matt to oversee the unloading.

On the way into the boiler-house the lorry from Arigna knocked over a gate-post. Reversing to avoid more damage the lorry knocked over the second gate-post.

The driver jumped out of his cab in a fluster.

"Keep this up," Matt said, "and we'll both lose our jobs."

"I'll pay for the damage," the driver offered.

"You needn't bother," Matt said.

"What?"

"I'm sick of this job anyhow," Matt said.

The driver shoved his cap back on his head and told Matt if he kept his mouth shut he'd find work in Arigna and good money into the bargain.

On the way to Arigna, Matt told the driver his father's name was Thomas Leyden. His father had worked as a stonemason, travelling around the limestone counties: Clare, Galway, Sligo and Roscommon. While his father was away, Matt looked after his mother, Mary McDonagh. He was the youngest in the family, and his pastimes were hunting and fishing, betting on the flat races in Roscommon and drinking. Other than being caught smoking woodbines during school hours, he was a good pupil and his teachers recommended he go on to agricultural college. But there was no money at home.

He got a job planting trees and shrubs around the new extension to Roscommon Hospital. Donkey and spadework mostly. With his brother-in-law, Packie, he double-jobbed as a hospital porter, wheeling corpses from the main building to the hospital mortuary. This was one of the reasons he decided to move on. "I didn't mind wheeling dead bodies to the mortuary, or God's waiting room, as Packie called it," he told the lorry driver. "But Packie liked to whistle while we were pushing the trolley."

The lorry crossed the cut-stone bridge in Carrick-on-Shannon and soon Matt got his first view of Arigna. Over the years the mineral reserves, first iron ore and then coal, brought all kinds of men to the district: industrialists, engineers, profiteers, speculators and labourers. The mines were the sole reason Arigna village came into existence and the place always had the aspect of a frontier settlement. But as the driver said to Matt, "There was money in Arigna when there was money nowhere."

Matt was arriving at a time when the coalmines were the living hub of the valley. Several different families had claims to the coal reserves in Arigna and the surrounding area, but the biggest and the most powerful employers in the area were the Layden family: old Mick Layden and his sons. The Laydens had grown from carpetbaggers in the wind-up of the Ascendancy estates to what locals regarded as millionaires. The Second World War brought further investment and expansion into larger mines with a bigger labour force and better wages. As one Arigna miner said, "That Harry Hitler; he should have been canonised."

Along with the mineral rights, the Laydens bought Castle Tennyson from the Earls of Kingston. They also acquired large amounts of land. Mick Layden had the biggest house in Arigna, with a grocery shop, post office and colliery offices under the one roof. A second substantial residence owned by the Layden family stood on the opposite side of the valley. It also overlooked the colliery yard where they graded and sold the company coal. Locals referred to these coal yards as the 'Siding'. A name left over from the days when a narrow-gauge railway line carried coal from the valley via the Cavan and Leitrim Railways. The Siding was also the site of a defunct iron ore smelting plant with its outbuildings, and the original iron foundry company houses were also owned by the Laydens.

. That casual chat with the lorry driver gave Matt the impression that the Layden family owned the valley, the homes and the jobs of everyone in it. Unfortunately, they were not related to Matt. But the driver explained that the coalminers and their employers had their own way of negotiating terms. Like the time Billy Keegan, an old miner working for the Laydens, said to a young fella shovelling coal at a fierce rate, "Can't you take it easy, they're millionaires." Billy never noticed who was standing behind him until Mick Layden said, "With the shower I have working for me I'd want to be a millionaire."

The life of the coalminer was hard, but there was work for the men of Arigna when 'having a job was as good as winning the Sweepstakes'. The pitmen worked a short day from eight in the morning until four in the evening, and a back shift from four until midnight. Sons followed fathers down the mines. This tight-knit dangerous work in the tunnels underground nurtured deep loyalties amongst the extended families of Arigna. Close-knit, hardworking, inter-married families beholden to their employers. Colliery workers.

When they got to Arigna Matt said good luck to the lorry driver. He took a walk around the village. Then he stopped for a drink in Flynn's pub. He was told about a dance on that night. Along with smoking, Matt had a habit of visiting dancehalls around the country. Especially the hops held in army huts bought cheap after the war and converted for peacetime use. The hops were good fun. But unlike the parish hall, the local priest got no part of the takings on the door and these out-of-the-way dances had a notoriously bad reputation amongst the clergy.

The cakewalk and strut of American Jazz and its hot brassy rhythms were condemned as the Devil's music. Respectable dance halls might allow the Zambezi but there were signs up saying 'No Jitterbugging.' And rumour said the Devil himself had been caught dancing to his own tunes. A good girl led astray at a hop one night looked down and spotted a cloven hoof prancing amongst the women's stilettos and the men's polished brogues. The Devil disappeared in a ball of flame through the floorboards the instant he was spotted, leaving the stink of sulphur in the air. Of course, the wilder the stories and the more the priests 'gave out stink from the altar' about the loose women and carnal temptations of these low haunts, the bigger the crowds the following week.

Even without a personal appearance by the Devil, there were plenty of genuine rogues at the hops: men on the lookout for women flustered by the hum of sweat and Brylcream, slicked hair and the fumes of the bottle of stout taken beforehand. And before asking a girl out to dance, Matt had been taught by his older brothers to use his Ronson or strike a match in the low light as a ploy to see if a girl was good-looking or not.

That night Matt stood outside a farmhouse at the upper end of Arigna valley in a place known as 'the turn out'. He had imagined he was going to a hop but he discovered a house-dance, or what the coalminers in Arigna called a 'porter spree'. He lit a cigarette and considered his predicament. He had nothing with him, only the couple of bob in his pocket, a packet of Woodbines, a cigarette lighter, a hair comb and the clothes on his back. And a voice inside his head, perhaps, that whispered: *"Don't stay too long in this country or it will capture you."*

Walking into the farmhouse kitchen, he found himself a silent onlooker amongst a crowd of colliery workers dressed in their best suits; strong and stout men in the habit of squatting down on their hunkers to talk or smoke a cigarette as if they were still under the low roof of a mineshaft. Flute music filled the crowded kitchen: the tunes of John McKenna played by a young man called Packie Duignan. And then a dance set played by the three Cryan brothers whose jobs in the dole office earned them the nickname Faith, Hope and Charity.

In the dim light, Matt spotted the twin sisters. Both women had permanents in their auburn hair and both wore imitation pearl necklaces. Two lively girls in cotton print dresses sprouting charms and sporting the stilettos they had carried in their hands to avoid scuffing or damaging them until they arrived at the house-dance.

He approached the two girls directly. He offered each of them a cigarette. The flint of his Ronson sparked. Holding up the flame he lit one girl's cigarette, then he lit the other, contrasting and comparing in the glow.

"Are you dancing?" he asked Nan.

"Are you asking?"

"I'm asking."

"I'm dancing."

She gave Lil her handbag to hold. She stood beside him on the flagstone kitchen floor. The music started. His hands were strong, his grip firm. He had the steps practiced. One-two-three, one-two-three; and then the quickstep together.

The next day, Matt approached the Laydens looking for work. Old Mick Layden hymned and hawed. He needed a man to look after the boiler-house as much as he needed a gardener. Boiler maintenance was no problem, Matt told him. He got the job. And the following week Matt moved to Arigna; an outsider whose trade stemmed from sunlight in a valley where other men spent their days labouring in the darkness underground.

We stopped the car on the side of Chapel Hill and got out. The parish priest, Father Tynan, paced the chapel yard, puffing on his pipe and inspecting the damage done to the church. He was talking to another man who stood on top of the wreck, shovelling gravel from the loaded truck.

When he saw my mother, Father Tynan broke off his tour of inspection to ask how was her sister Lil?

"She's had a setback," Nan said.

"She has a lot ahead of her," he said. "I'll say a prayer."

We stood looking over the cemetery wall at the wreckage.

"Who was driving?" Nan asked. "Anyone we know?"

"A young fella," said Father Tynan. "He had a lucky escape I hear. Just a broken arm."

I couldn't help feeling sorry for the owners of the lorry, and for the driver who would have to answer for this accident. But it seemed foolhardy to take a lorry that big with a load that heavy down a gradient that steep.

"What was he doing driving down Chapel Hill?" I asked.

"He was new," said Father Tynan. "He didn't know the area."

"He's learning," the Arigna man beside him said.

THE LONGEST RIVER

Matt rented a house on the banks of the Arigna River. The rent was low because the house was haunted. One night he was having a drink at the kitchen table with a couple of pitmen when the hall door slammed shut. The pitmen got a fright, but Matt said, "Don't mind that fella. He passes through here this time every night."

Matt kept a bachelor's house. The settee pulled up close to the fire, a Foxford wool blanket thrown over the cushions, a black Labrador gun-dog called Chalky for company, and a valve radio with big round knobs that Matt could adjust using his toes as he lay on the settee with his socks off after a hard day in the garden.

He was working full-time for the Laydens. Apple trees, pear trees and plum trees were planted and blackcurrant bushes and gooseberry canes set. He trained and pruned into order the oldest and the wildest varieties of rambling rose, and cultivated new varieties. While the dwelling house took priority, some heat was diverted from the coal-fired boiler to a new glasshouse. And after a special trip to meet the head gardener in Lissadell House in Sligo, Matt returned with the first tomato plants ever to be grown in the valley.

In the evenings he went fishing. One evening he was fishing for trout with a pitman called Gerald Wynne. Gerald lost his float. Matt didn't have a spare float, but he spotted an empty porter bottle at the edge of the river.

Gerald retrieved the bottle. The cork had been shoved down into the bottle. Gerald got a brain wave. He looped a length of fishing line to cradle the cork and ease it out straight. But every attempt failed to get the cork out of the bottle.

"I need something stronger," Gerald said, "like a piece of wire or a knitting needle to make a harpoon."

"What do you want?" Matt asked. "A harpoon or a cork?"

"The cork."

Matt took the bottle and broke it against a rock. He picked up the cork.

"Smart arse," said Gerald.

*

On Lough Allen Matt went fishing with Gerald Wynne and Jim Early who kept a boat on the lake. They stopped on a small island. A storm blew up and they were forced to spend the night on Inishmagrath Island. While they weathered out the squall, they found a tin can and boiled seagull eggs for their supper. Then they sat around a driftwood fire and Jim Early told Matt about the flagstone on the island that floated out across the lake and stopped at Dead Man's Point to collect the dead and ferry them back to the island for burial in the grounds of the ruined abbey. Long ago, the Abbey was just one of seven churches that miraculously appeared overnight in the district.

With the flames from their campfire bouncing shadows off the walls they showed Matt the human skulls nested in the gaps in the masonry of the ruined abbey. He was all for bringing a skull home. He said it would be company for the ghost in his house.

But Gerald Wynne told him about the woman from Dublin who took a skull off the island. She thought the skull would make a novelty sugar bowl at her dinner parties. The boatman warned her not to steal it but she wouldn't listen. When she finally put the upturned skull on the dinner table in front of her guests a blood red stain spread through the sugar.

Matt put back the skull.

*

Over the winter Matt started to build his own boat. By the middle of the following summer the seams were caulked and the wooden rowboat ready for its maiden voyage. He got the boat delivered on a coal lorry to the shores of Lough Allen.

The timber boat was an apprentice job with leaks in the joinery. Once the keel of the boat scraped free from the shallows he climbed on board. But even Chalky the Labrador was reluctant to follow. Normally obedient, Chalky stood shivering and whining on the lakeshore looking down at the boat taking in water and then looking up at Matt the boat builder.

"Suit yourself," said Matt, shoving out.

Chalky dashed through the lily pads and flung himself on board, shaking off lake water from his nose to his tail. More water welled in between the boards. But after a certain amount of soakage the joints began to weld.

They headed out onto the lake. Chalky sat up front to navigate. Matt sat on the short cross-seat. They were the only ones out on the lake that day. Nobody would spot them if the boat went down. And yet Matt cherished this isolation. He had the day off work and he was accountable to nobody. His garden was in order. The tomato plants in the greenhouse had been watered and the windows in the roof were propped open to relieve the sultry heat. Tonight he was meeting Nan. Ahead of him would be marriage, children, responsibilities.

But for now he was a free man.

Insects darted over the still lake with the countryside cloistered in haze. A single heron perched on a sun-hot stone. The dog kept watch. With only the softest lapping of lake water against the boards everything beyond the clumsily made craft looked distant, serene, hypnotic. The lake stretched before him but he drew in the oars and closed his eyes, at ease with the fluid insistence of the current. Man and vessel being carried by the longest river.

DREAM PURCHASE

It was Nan's idea to show him Castle Tennyson. Matt was glad to have his job working for the Laydens, but the pay was poor and he was looking for another source of income. The vacant castle grounds contained a walled garden with an orchard and a solid fuel boiler and heated glasshouse that might be restored. They walked the castle grounds, weighing up their potential and watching the play of light between the specimen trees, the sweep of the long avenue and the placing of the castle next the lake.

"How did they do it?" Nan asked, enthralled by the beauty of the landscaping, the planting scheme and the specimen trees imported from the most exotic corners of the Empire.

"Money is great manure," Matt said.

Having scouted the estate, Nan suggested they lease one wing of the castle to live in while they revived the walled garden, the orchard and the greenhouse. With Matt's gardening know-how and her farming ability they could start a market garden business.

Nan never slept a wink that night planning the move. Impossible as it seemed, she was on the brink of realising a childhood fantasy. Nan and her sister Lil had been in their teens when they first worked up the nerve to cycle out to Castle Tennyson. It stood barely three miles away from the home place on the mountain, but the castle was a forbidden and mysterious place. A domain as off limits to both girls as the outlandish wealth it symbolised.

Their father, Henry Joe McDermot, had carried boxes of homemade butter on his back across the mountain to sell in the butter market in Sligo to pay his rent to the castle owners, the Earls of Kingston, while his young family ate dry bread. He sold bacon and ate plain potatoes for the same reason.

Nan had heard stories at home about the time the Kingstons'

coach-and-four pulled up at the entrance to the estate. The gatekeeper was sick and his 14-year-old daughter opened the gates. The following day, word came down from the castle to have the girl's hair chopped off and to dress her in rags. The Lady of the house had caught the look in her husband's eye, and she knew exactly what it meant for her and for the girl. And from stories whispered amongst neighbours by the fireside Nan and Lil learned how a local priest finally stood and wiped his shoes on the doorstep of Castle Tennyson swearing, "One day the grass will grow over the monuments of tyrants".

By the time the two girls cycled up the avenue, the curse the priest had drawn down that day on the castle had been largely fulfilled. The gatehouse which had been carved out of the sandstone escarpment at the entrance to the estate stood empty and windowless. After the long avenue the castle loomed on a height, its windows dark and the grounds returned to rough pasture.

Finding the empty coach tunnel, the girls looked down through the iron grating into the passage that encircled the house like a covered moat, allowing servants to come and go unseen. They admired the stained glass panels around the private chapel door and the stone-carved coat of arms high up on the wall. They peeped in the windows at the dumb-waiter, the cast-iron central heating system, the marble fireplaces and the ballroom with the beautiful wrought-iron spiral stairs, the fabulous white domed ceiling and the heavy and ornate plaster cornice.

"One day," Nan told Lil, "I'm going to live in this castle."

The castle changed hands, but it was Mick Layden and the Arigna coal mining company who took over the estate to secure the Kingston mineral rights. Soon after the Laydens took possession they began to dismantle the castle for their own ends. The cut-stone steps were taken from the front lawn and installed outside the chapel in Arigna. Marble fireplaces were removed and transferred to their own homes. The finest oak panelling was used to prop up shafts in the coalmines.

The fabric of the castle suffered further depredations. At one point the castle was used as a temporary barracks and the interior altered to accommodate the Army Construction Corps. Astonishing forests of dry rot flourished behind the stucco-plastered walls fashioned by Italian craftsmen. Lead went missing from the roof and the rain leaked in. Even the daffodils in the grounds were spirited away to the household gardens of Arigna.

But enough survived to allow Nan to hope.

Early the next day, Nan and Matt presented themselves at Mick Layden's front door. Nan was all dressed up and Matt wore his best sports jacket. They were led into a front room. A coal fire burned in the grate. Tea was brought in. Old Mick Layden listened to their proposal.

When they finished he said it was a great idea. But did they understand that the number of chimneys and the area of the roof dictated the Government rates on a residential building? The only way to avoid payment was to leave the building unoccupied. They could live in one wing of the castle if they liked, but they would have to pay the full rates. Nan and Matt went home and looked at the figures. The overheads would be crippling. Their dream purchase slipped out of reach.

Without tenants, the castle sunk further into ruin. The rain-damaged ceilings began to collapse, and the weight of the one that fell brought down the floor below. Everything of value was looted and scavenged from the decaying hulk. Graffiti covered the walls. Sheep rambled the interior. And looking at the castle in its final ruin Nan remarked to Matt, "I'll say this much for the Kingstons; they might have been tyrants, but they had taste."

ENGLAND IN THE '50'S

They headed for England. Matt went first. Reluctantly, Nan followed him over on the boat. Her mother and father said England would be her ruination. And privately she told her sister Lil she might be better off going to America. But America seemed so far away. And what if she went to America and didn't like it? She'd never get back.

Nobody she ever heard had anything good to say about England or the English. And yet, on the day she sailed, the crowd of men and women from every part of Ireland packed the deck. One young man stood shivering inside an overcoat twice too big for him, with a safety pin holding a label on his chest. The address he had to find in England was handwritten in block letters on the label. He couldn't read or write but he had instructions from his mother to show the label to people until he got to where he was going. Nan never found out if he made it, but for the first time in her life she felt grateful to her schoolteachers for the grain of education they'd beaten into her.

She found London a strange place of mournful Thames River fogs and grey monumental buildings in a city splotched with red double-decker buses, red call-boxes and red pillar-boxes. A city of gas meters, tripe and chintz covers in the boarding houses and landladies obsessed with Littlewoods' Pools. There were notices in the public toilets warning women against V.D. And she met some queer types on the Underground, talking to themselves and shouting in the tunnels. A lot of them were disturbed by the War. She got palpitations and found it hard to breathe going down the stairs to the deeper tunnels, so she stopped using the Underground and went everywhere by bus. She preferred to see where she was going.

Matt couldn't find work as a gardener. He had to take a job on the buildings. Nan answered the advertisements in the London evening papers and finally she was offered a job on a production line in Plessies.

There she soldered components into the chassis of valve radios midst the tang of flux and delicately applied hot metal. Work that to her mind was child's play after the drudgery on the farm at home.

She was barely a wet week working when a troublemaker on the line in Plessies threatened to bring the whole place out on strike. He wouldn't lift the radios off his bench after he'd done with them and stack them on the shelf overhead. He said he had a bad back and it wasn't his job and he'd call in the union. None of the women wanted any trouble. The English women were powerful workers and they were delighted to be able to keep on their jobs after the War. They said, "He won't listen to us. But you're Irish. You got a temper. And you let 'm 'avit, dear."

Nan rounded on the buck causing all the trouble and finished up telling him, "If we had the likes of you at home we'd tie an apron on you and call you Nancy." The other women cheered and laughed him out of the place. And they had no more trouble after that.

Harold McMillan told everyone, "You've never had it so good." And Nan often felt guilty collecting her wage packet at the end of the week. She took home twice what her father earned working in the coal-mines.

When she went to England, Nan's mother and father were afraid of only one thing - that she might end up a Protestant. She never lost her faith, but when she spotted an Englishman at ten o'clock at night leave the right money and take a newspaper from a stand, and only the one paper, she thought of the crowd at home - how they'd have swept money, papers, the lot. England taught her that she could be a good Christian without having to be seen every Sunday cracking her knees at the altar.

Like the other Irish men labouring in England, Matt had to go wherever he could find work: what the Irish lads called 'following the mixer'. He ended up working for the winter on the motorways outside Coventry. He didn't like it, but he pitied the poor Jamaicans. They were only landed in England and they were perished with the cold.

The gangers were rough. They gave the men under them fierce abuse. And the Irish gangers were as bad as any. Matt pulled up outside a house one morning in a builder's truck. A woman stuck her head out a window and said, "I'm surprised at you men working today. The Queen has just given birth to a son." The ganger roared, "I don't care if she had a litter of *bonhams* - get this truck unloaded."

The builder's digs were dog rough. God be good to him, Gerald

Wynne, his friend from Arigna, shared the same digs with Matt. The food was terrible. Heads of cow cabbage boiled in a galvanised iron bucket with slugs and all. One evening the landlady gave them boiled fish. She caught Gerald looking at the bit of fish floating in a pool of water on his plate. "Is there something the matter with your dinner?" she asked. Said Gerald "I'm waiting for the tide to go out." Setting the table another evening, she dropped a fork on the floor and said to Matt, "We'll have a stranger calling." "Must be the butcher," he said.

But you couldn't always blame the landladies. They were dealing with a horrid rough crowd that didn't know or want any better. You'd find cow dung on the pillowcase left by the last tenant, straight off the cattle boat. And in London you'd see them getting on the bus: the fighting Irish with the shirt outside the trousers.

One time Nan saw a bunch of Teddy Boys taking up the whole of Islington High Street. They were jig-acting and pushing everyone out of the way. This big Kerryman came up behind them with a ton of cement on his size 18 boots and he gave the ringleader the best kick up the arse any man ever got. She had to laugh, but he was looking for trouble. And every night, a fight started in the Irish pubs. Matt and herself got fed up handing over money for collections to pay for broken windows or to get this fella or that fella out of jail.

If Matt wanted to get off the buildings to work as a gardener they would have to go where the big shots lived. Every Sunday and free day they went out together to see what was available. In the good areas they put on an accent at the bus stop and said to the people beside them: "It's the chauffeur's day off." They finally got a place in Surbiton, working for a Mrs. Smith White. They lived in the gatehouse. When the crocus and daffodil bulbs came up in the spring it was beautiful.

Matt worked under the head gardener, Luke. He opened the glasshouse and the vinery in the summer. Old Luke didn't like Matt being in charge of the soft fruits. But he didn't know enough about them himself. He tried to hide it, but there was friction the whole time.

The cook said she was Swiss but Nan felt certain she was German. You couldn't blame her saying she was Swiss, what with the War and all. The rest of her fell everywhere but she had a lovely face. She made garlic bread for lunch and taught Nan the recipe. She showed Nan how to use the coffee percolator. When the owners were away, she took Nan through the house to show her the lovely antique furniture in the dinning room, the billiard room and the gun room. Matt had mixed feelings about the gentry, but he couldn't hide how much he admired the Purdy. A beautiful shotgun, he said. The real McCoy.

Ted Slater was the young lad in charge of the gun room. Nan liked Ted. He was full of fun. Miss Borton, the head housekeeper, had thick, curly hair and black eyelashes. One day, looking at Miss Borton turning the handle on her big iron mincer in her full regalia, Ted remarked to Nan, "She's like a doll that you leave down and the eyes close."

Ted came from a very good family but his ambition was to be a gunsmith. He took Nan and Matt to see the place where the guns were made. She laughed when she heard the name: Oxshot. Ted was a sportsman and made his own split-cane fishing rods and tied his own flies. He had a great pair of hands. Doing his National Service he held onto a grenade too long and lost four fingers. After the accident Ted disappeared to become a gamekeeper in a remote part of Scotland.

She missed Ted. He had tried hard to make a proper English couple out of Matt and her. "Annie," he said, for he never called her Nan. "Annie, dear, you can't walk into a shop and ask for a spool of thread. It's a reel of cotton over here. And, 'Arf of brown'," Ted teased Matt. " 'Arf of brown', not a glass of stout." But as soon as their first child was born, Matt came straight out with it. "I don't want my son growing up in this country," he said.

Nan put away the most precious things she'd gathered in England, and the tears streamed down her face when she looked at the pile of tea chests ready for shipping back to Ireland.

When Matt asked her why she was so upset, she said, "England was good to me."

A DOG FOR COMPANY

Matt hated confinement and was happy to be home from England. Back in Arigna in his gardening job he took up fishing and shooting again and trained a new hunting dog, a crusty fox terrier called Harvey, who also became the self-appointed guardian of the family.

By now, Matt and Nan had three children, with a gap of two to three years between each of us. I was the middle child. While my older brother, Terry, spent hours each day digging holes in the ash-pit beside the house – making a racetrack for his Dinky and Matchbox toy cars – Harvey rested his head on his front paws, one eye charily keeping lookout as my mother hung out to dry the never-ending lines of dungarees and vests, terrycloth nappies and cot bedding.

If Terry was an easygoing five-year-old who totally ignored my existence as long as I left his toy cars alone, my baby brother Dermot was as contrary as a bag of weasels. When he found his bottle too hot or too cold, he flung it away. On warm days, anybody passing Dermot's enormous blue hooded pram in the yard had to look out for low-flying bottles. But Harvey was always there to fetch them back, and lick up any splattered milk or baby food.

From the time I first started to rise out a crawl, Harvey tolerated my grabbing hold of his short tail to pull myself upright. Then, with my hands rested on his back he would move off, walking slowly for me to keep up. Before long the two of us could be seen parading in and out the garden path, Harvey walking patiently alongside me in case I lost my balance. And so began my love of long walks with only a dog for company.

It also instigated a lifelong habit of walking myself into trouble, starting at age four. I was out the fields one day on my own when a sinister-looking tramp in a battered topcoat, dark glasses and felt hat with the brim turned down stepped into my path, blocking the way.

"Where are you going?" he growled.

I stood looking at him, knowing I was alone except for the dog. But for some strange reason Harvey refused to growl back. With no other help in sight, I took off in the direction of home as fast as my little fat legs could carry me.

Though I was terrified the tramp might be chasing me, I slowed after the first dash and looked over my shoulder to see if Harvey was all right. I saw the tramp, hunkered down and talking to my bodyguard. And if I had been as smart as the dog that day, I too would have recognised my father.

Dressing up as a tramp was a ploy agreed with my mother to frighten me out of the habit of wandering off on my own 'exploring'. Though my mother thought it a terrible thing to put the frighteners on a small child she was at her wits' end. Every time she turned her back I wandered out of the house, whereupon she had to drop everything and go running after me.

By the time I got home that day I was as white as a sheet. My mother was waiting, and she petted and coaxed me to tell her what had happened, so that she might explain the dangers of wandering off on my own. But I lowered my chin, tugged at my earlobe and never opened my mouth.

A short time later a travelling fun-fair stopped in the village. The minute my mother turned her back I was out the door and off to see the amusements. There seemed to be nobody about as I went around behind the line of parked caravans before the fairground. Out of the silence a guard-dog pounced - an Alsatian, frothing from the tongue and bounding towards me with the speed and deadliness of a sprung trap. I froze at the realisation that animal hurt was about to be done to me. The dog was almost on top of me when Harvey jumped into his path.

It was a savage fight. The two dogs rolling in the dirt, stripped teeth chewing at each other's throats, a kill-or-die look in their maddened eyes. I roared for help, knowing it would be my fault if Harvey got killed. But the owners came running from the fairground and broke up the fight by throwing a bucket of water over the two dogs. Harvey's ear was torn and there was blood around his throat, but he had kept off the bigger dog until I could be rescued.

Both trembling, I hugged my wounded champion to shield him against further harm, the tears coming hot and wet and Harvey panting like a bellows. I wanted him to know I understood how close I had come to being mauled, maimed or worse. But Harvey would not relax his guard. He kept looking past me, his eyes fixed on the panting predator that my earliest exploring had found such a short distance beyond the creaturely protection of the nursery.

THE FIRST GARDEN

The garden where my father worked was called 'The Plot'. The plot provided his employers with fresh fruit and vegetables. The surplus fed his family. It was not far from the bungalow where we lived and it was a treat to be allowed to visit it. To keep out pests, a chain-link fence surrounded the plot. This fence seemed enormously high to me. Whenever I stepped through the gate into the maintained atmosphere of the plot, I felt the air on that side of the fence as different to the air on the other side, a boundary beyond which the ordinary world stopped and inklings of pure mystery began.

The plot bordered the Arigna River and my father often brought a fishing rod to work. If he saw a curl on the water or the ripple of a trout rising in the turn-hole below the bridge, he would put down his garden tools, pick up his rod and delicately cast a fly - to play a whim, to tease a fish and bring home a trout for the evening tea.

Beside the plot stood a yard with old rolling stock, left behind after the narrow-gauge railway line into the valley shut down. As I got older I converted one of the timber-frame carriages into a playhouse. One summer I began to hear a strange scratching sound. I couldn't place the noise until my father found the source: wasps chewing the timber sides of the wooden carriage with their strong mandibles to make paper for their nest.

It enthralled me to hear my father use words like mandible, pulp and regurgitate. And it gave him pleasure to improve my grasp of the natural world, pointing to the predatory weevils in the clay and the colouring-book bright ladybirds on the leaves.

As I grew older he would explain the difference between onion sets and shallots and the distinction between hardy annuals and perennials. He gave me an additional language of antique garden weights and measures: the linear inch, foot, and yard; the surveyor's, link, pole, perch, chain and rod; the Troy grain and pennyweight; the Avoirdupois ounce, pound and hundredweight; the liquid gill, pint, quart and gallon. A beautiful, granary-rich language that perfectly fitted parcels of turned earth, palmfuls of dry seeds and wheat grains. And he spoke a further garden vocabulary too, as moist and yielding on the tongue as bruised fruit, words like tuber, tendril, succulent, legume, and loam: supple and pleasing descriptions that harmonised with my feelings for the natural world.

My father promoted my education, telling me it was a passport out of hardship. But I was still at an age where learning relied on the impact of experience on my immediate senses. And one of my earliest visits to the plot stood out from all the rest.

On that day my father had taken me by the hand through the gate into the plot, across that chain-link boundary into the territory of wonder. Together we walked between the raised beds and planted drills, the neat lines of plants so evidently in his care.

Bright summer sunlight scattered through the leaves. Only the passing butterflies disturbed the still air. This luscious calm concentrated the undersong of the garden, from the kingfisher cheeping along the riverbank, to the scraping of the grasshoppers in the undergrowth.

My father hunkered down next to me and we started to pick garden peas. The first flush. Enough for an early dinner. Following his example, I reached into the cool greenery and plucked and popped a tender pod open. I scooped the juicy peas out and ate from the palm of my hand.

My God! The sweetness. The flavour. The perfect delight of that moment in the garden where my father had a measure and a name for every plant and creature. Where he laboured each day to transform fallow clay into cultivated ground.

INDUSTRIAL ACTION

"When they were laying the cable on the sea floor for the first transatlantic phone line, they found the iron rims belonging to the wheels of the carts that brought coal from Arigna to America," my father said as I held the bridle of the ass and cart and we stood by the weighbridge at Arigna Collieries Limited. It was a wet Saturday afternoon and a line of donkeys and carts waited at the weighbridge, together with Volkswagen Beetle cars towing small trailers, and grey Ferguson diesel-20 tractors with transport boxes linked to the back. From all around there came a constant clatter of conveyor belts and the ring of navvy shovels, the ooze of coal dust, oil and rain, and the towering rumble of heavy industry.

According to the prophecies of Saint Colmcille, when the biblical Antichrist came to our part of the world, he would 'lower the hills and raise the hollows'. But the disproportionate amount of ash produced burning the local coal did the same job; people said that for every bucket load of Arigna coal you burned you took away two buckets full of ashes. The coal was supposed to be screened for impurities before it passed down the chutes into the bunkers. But you could easily find the man on the screen sound asleep in a chair in front of the conveyor belt, lulled to sleep in the radiance of a red hot iron stove where the best nuggets of coal blazed.

You weighed in when you arrived and weighed out when you had a full load. Working for the Laydens as a gardener and a labourer, a fuel allocation supplemented my father's wage. And over by the bunkers that day we joined the other customers and employees picking through the coal heaps to make up a load. My father got out a shovel but mostly we hand-picked the coal to avoid the slates and lumps of low-grade coal that would never ignite beyond a dull ball of ash. Even in my small hand the good coal felt surprisingly light, and looked at close up, the best nuggets glistened like oil on the surface of water. Slates were heavy and grey.

When we had the cart loaded we returned to the weighbridge and the office where Teresa Guihen watched for trickery: rocks hidden while weighing in and then dumped before loading up with coal. She issued the dockets, calibrated the weight and named the price for the nuts, slack or lump coal, the briquettes or the broken briquettes rejected from the new 'bagging' plant. "She might let us away with a bit extra," my father said, "if we licked up to her."

The company were putting a fleet of new Lorries on the road, painted a uniform red, but an aerial rope was still in use. Iron pylons extended from the coal yards towards the mountain and the coalmines and slag heaps above the valley. Unlike the Welsh and English mines, the coal in Arigna was drift-mined in the mountains and not excavated from deep shafts in the valleys. The aerial rope was a cable car or funicular system, by which one set of loaded buckets entered the valley while the empty buckets were hauled back up the mountain to the mines. Sometimes a bucket came off. At the best of times the aerial rope made a fearful clatter. People were afraid of the aerial rope, especially crossing on foot underneath where it spanned the public road.

The aerial rope was also a scapegoat for a deeper tension between the people of the valley, the miners and their employers. A strike that began unofficially before Christmas 1968 had escalated into all-out industrial action that lasted into the spring of 1969. This strike was the cause of great bitterness, especially amongst the 250 coal-miners working for the Laydens. The labour force had been left penniless over Christmas, passing the winter without fuel to heat their homes or to cook their meals. The spokesmen for the miners were labelled 'a few troublemakers' and accused of subversion and of trying to intimidate scab labourers and strike-breakers. Accusations of blocking coal supplies to the County Home and the District Hospital were raised. As the strike continued, every able-bodied miner marched the 12 miles from Arigna to Carrick-on-Shannon to gain support from 'the working men and women of Ireland' and their 'just fight'. Gathered with our classmates along the sides of the road, we cheered the striking miners as they marched out of the valley. After a stop in Leitrim

Village for 'light refreshments', a rally convened outside the courthouse in Carrick-on-Shannon, calling public attention to the demands of the miners for better working conditions and a five-day working week.

I was too young to really grasp what was going on, but I was sensitive enough to the tensions in the aftermath of the strike to be wetting the bed at night without knowing why. Though the strike had been settled, the feelings of division and resentment caused by it were still palpable that day as I stood at the colliery weighbridge, while my father haggled over what he owed along with his fuel allowance. Suddenly word started to go around that Brendan Layden, a company director and a son of old Mick Layden, was going to demonstrate the safety of the aerial rope.

The aerial rope clattered nosily as the buckets ahead of the one supposedly carrying Brendan Layden entered the Siding. We stood and watched what was at first a dark speck high up on the mountain. Finally we spotted a figure standing in an empty bucket descending on the steel cable spanning the valley. If the bucket came off, it would more than likely jump the aerial rope at a pylon. The bucket rattled and clunked past two pylons. There was one pylon to go. The motor hauling the line seemed to hiccup. The bucket with Brendan Layden teetered. Then it was over the last pylon. It crossed the public road and Brendan Layden entered the coal sales yard waving. Whistles and cheers from the colliery workers and the customers picking coal by hand from the bunkers below met the heroic company director. Smiling and waving heartily up at his employer's high wire act, the colliery worker standing next to my father said, "It's a pity he didn't break his neck."

*

We were living in a bungalow that came with my father's job. This housing concession was another reason for his low wages. The bungalow was built around a timber frame and the outer walls had weatherproofed tiles. It was an unusual house for that period: a prefabricated forerunner of the bungalow invasion, and it stood alone in the field next to the Siding at the centre of the village. While it was an exceptionally snug house it felt exposed - exposed to view and to obligation.

In the field where the bungalow stood there was a curious looking rock. A compact and dull red rock pitted with corrosion, it drove my toy compass needle wild. In fact this rock was an ingot of solid pig-iron that had been allowed to solidify in the bed of the furnace of the Arigna Iron Foundry after it closed for the last time. A ricochet from the valley's troubled industrial past.

The school geography books said Ireland produced only three things; shoes, grass and molasses. There were no minerals in Ireland. The passing of the glaciers had scraped the country bare of its mineral riches.

Yet the iron ore deposits in the Arigna locality had been worked as far back as the 15th century. The mountain on the opposite side of Lough Allen was originally called *Sliabh an Ierin*, the Iron Mountain. In her book *Gods and Fighting Men*, Lady Gregory said that this mountain was the first landing place of the mythical Tuatha de Dannan tribe in Ireland, whose boat arrived in a cloud and settled on the top of the far mountain. I mentioned this piece of information to a local coal-miner once, who looked towards the rust-coloured mountain across the lake and said that either Lady Gregory got her facts - or the Tuathan de Dannan their directions - wrong.

By the 1600s, the various iron works of Sir Charles Coote employed over 3,000 men in the district. Not one of his foundry workers was Irish; on no account were Irishmen to be employed lest they learn the secrets of the iron industry. Understandably, the Coote iron works were destroyed in a rebellion in 1641.

Not long after the battle of the Boyne, in 1690, Patrick Reynolds established a furnace in nearby Drumshanbo in County Leitrim. He supplied iron to the first East India Company ship built in Limerick. He employed Irish workers - the father of the composer and harpist Turlough O'Carolan was a foundry man who moved with his family from Nobber in County Meath. However, when the surrounding timber supplies ran out, around 1765, Reynolds closed his foundry business.

Soon after, the O'Reilly brothers, Thomas, Patrick and Andrew, began iron smelting at Furnace Hill outside Drumshanbo, near where a later canal meets Lough Allen today. Coal deposits discovered two miles west of Lough Allen fuelled their furnaces. Along with the coalmines owned by the O'Reilly brothers, coal mining was carried out by Colonel Thomas Tennyson. It was Colonel Tennyson who called his castle at Kilronan, 'that oasis in the mountain wilderness'. By the 1800s, Colonel Tennyson's mining operation on Kilronan Mountain was going strong, while the Archbishop of

Tuam was said to maintain a rival mine further down the valley.

The O'Reilly brothers also undertook the construction of an extensive iron foundry in Arigna. It was a disastrous move financially. Few traces of their foundry remained, but older people still referred to the land beside the chapel in Arigna as 'the reservoir field'. And my walks with the dog often took in the ruins of the reservoir wall that stood in the field behind the bungalow.

When the O'Reilly brothers failed to secure grant aid from Parliament, their foundry in Arigna went bankrupt. The banker, Peter Latouche, for what he considered the bargain price of £25,000, bought the iron works, having previously bankrolled the foundry for up to £10,000. Despite further heavy investment, the iron works closed. Latouche retired to his estate at Bellevue near Greystones in Dublin. One day, showing a visitor around the grounds, he pointed to a wrought-iron gate made in Arigna and said: 'You never saw a gate that cost any man so much.'

An attempt to revive the Arigna Iron Works in 1824 appears to have been a fraudulent device to fool shareholders in London. For a time, however, English foundry workers and Scottish coal-miners poured into the district. A newspaper article reported that Arigna resembled, 'a little colony in a new country.'

The extraction of Arigna iron ore deposits was never viable on a large scale, and the coal found in the district was considered too brittle for wide commercial use. But in 1888, the Arigna Mining Company was incorporated to supply coal to the Cavan and Leitrim Light Railways. In a mutually advantageous arrangement, the chairman of both enterprises was the Earl of Kingston, a descendant of Colonel Tennyson, and heir to his mineral rights.

In what would have been an advantageous move for both interests, it was proposed to extend the light railway system from the nearest terminus to the coalmines. This idea caused outrage amongst the carters, who were paid to transport the coal the one and a half mile journey from the Arigna mines to the station house at Mount Allen.

It was only through the Board of Works, using the Defence of the Realm Act, that an extension was begun in 1918. This branch line into Arigna opened on the 2nd of June 1920. For nine years the line remained the property of the Government, but Cavan and Leitrim Railways managed it. In effect, Cavan and Leitrim Railways were subsidised by the

Government to manage a service that provided their own railway company with coal supplied by their own mining company. And the Government further reimbursed Cavan and Leitrim Railways for running what was on paper a loss-making service. In 1925, the Cavan and Leitrim Railway Company was taken over by Great Southern Railways. Unsurprisingly, they bought their coal from Wales.

As the Earl of Kingston wound down the Arigna Coal Mining Company, the Layden family began to take over. They consolidated their position as the largest mining interest in the area with a contract to supply subsidised coal to the new Irish Government-built power station on the shores of Lough Allen.

By the time Matt and Nan moved into the bungalow, the Laydens were experimenting with alternative uses for the remaining coal reserves, the quality of which was steadily declining. A method had been devised to compress hot pitch, sealed in a jacket of coal-dust, to make solid fuel ovoids or briquettes. First, the imported pitch had to be unloaded from the boat at the docks in Sligo and transported by lorry to Arigna.

As the Dockers and colliery workers shovelled this shiny residue of tar distillation they developed a mysterious burn on their hands, arms and faces. After only a day working on the docks my father came home with his arms burnt and a livid face.

I had been born in 1960, the year the French tested their first atomic bomb and the British launched their first atomic submarine, *Dreadnought*. Two years later the world had come to the brink of nuclear war after the Russians installed missiles with atomic warheads in Cuba. I also knew from my schoolbooks that Marie Curie extracted radium from pitchblende. Suddenly it looked as if Arigna's long industrial history had finally entered the atomic age.

When the pitch first arrived, my father and the other colliery workers had no idea it could be so harmful. But after their hands and faces began to burn they refused to shovel any more pitch, especially in a confined space.

The man in charge was Michael Layden, a brother of Brendan.

"Get the hell out of me way," he warned my father when he and the other colliery workers downed tools. Then he grabbed my father's shovel and began to shovel the hot payload by himself. He finished the job unassisted, but he wasn't seen for a week afterwards. Meals were sent up to

his room. He couldn't show his face. It was said, "The skin fell off him."
And after the eruptions?

It turned out that a reaction between the pitch dust and human
sweat caused the colliery workers' skin to burn; not radiation. The more you
sweated, especially in the confined and dusty space of a ship's hold or a
coalbunker, the worse you got burned.

My theory about mysterious atomic particles in the pitch was off
beam but the pace of industry in Arigna was accelerated by this volatile fuel
import. My mother was looking out the kitchen window of the bungalow
when the mechanical shovel drove up to the bunker full of pitch. Its
loading bucket and hydraulic arms could do the work of twenty labouring
men without side-effects. Neither grateful nor ungrateful, it was strong,
untiring and obedient.

JULY, 1969

The summer twilight lingered in the west as I waited for the rising of the moon. I was a devoted follower of the Apollo space programme, and the night before I had been allowed to stay up late to watch astronaut Neil Armstrong leave the impression of his boot on the moon.

The light dwindled. And when the first star pierced the clear night sky, I invoked a secret wish:

Star light, star bright,
I wish I may, I wish I might,
Have the wish I wish tonight.

As the darkness increased, the electric lights came on in the valley, in the farmhouses, the outbuildings and the colliery workers cottages of the North Roscommon coalfields of Arigna. A glow of light also sprang from the doorway of the barn where our neighbour, Billy Keegan, had arrived to do the milking. A short time later we heard the rattle in the dusk as Billy, who had been delayed in the pub, tripped over his galvanised iron buckets. "One small step for man…" I said. I heard my father laugh, as the glow of a burning match lit up his face and his cigarette smoke infused the night air.

Across the valley the headlights of the cars and the motorbikes taking the coal-miners home from the back-shift in the Arigna mines descended the side of the mountain going down Chapel Hill. In the glow from his cigarette I saw my father watching the crowd pull up outside the pub, where the new illuminated sign for Double Diamond shone its tantalizing message from the brewery.

He turned his back on the pub then, and together we looked up. More stars had appeared, and we squinted in the half-light at our map of the summer constellations, a star-map printed in the Saturday newspaper and cut out and kept by my father.

47

With his index finger pointing the direction overhead, he joined the dots of light into patterns and recited the names: Cassiopeia and the Pleiades, the Big Dipper also called Ursa Major, and the North or the Pole Star.

But my eyes now were on the lit-up edges of the clouds above the far mountain. The brightness increased and over the rim of the mountain the moon came up. A moon that looked the same as the night before, its face aglow and its mystery undimmed. And yet, to my mind, it was different. The Eagle had landed. The United State of America, in the name of all humankind, had staked a claim on that lunar surface with a flag raised over the Sea of Tranquility. And as we stood there in the transformed moonlight, it seemed that in the years to come there was nowhere curiosity and imagination and our most heartfelt wishes couldn't take us.

THE GLASS WOMAN

PART ONE

I

Teresa phoned from America. She said she had found a cure for her sister Lil's cancer. Looking up cancer information on the Internet, Teresa had stumbled on a method to boost Lil's immune system. The treatment was only available in Canada. But for a price the company would forward the product.   In less than a week a packet arrived addressed to my mother. She passed the packet on to me to examine the contents.

The customs declaration label on the outside of the brown padded envelope said it contained a medical lecture. Out first came a video describing the product and how to administer it. Then a cardboard box with two glass bottles full of a clear liquid called 714X: a compound to repair the body, improve appetite, give more energy and boost the immune system.

So far so good. And I had no qualms about employing any medicine as long as it didn't interfere with Lil's current treatment and her current treatment didn't interfere with it.

Feeling more material in plastic bubble-wrap at the bottom, I shook the packet. But when I saw what fell out, I froze, the sensation taking me back more than 30 years to the day I had to line up with my classmates outside the headmaster's office in the national school.

Word came down the line there was a nurse visiting our school. And when my turn came to step into the master's office, there really was a nurse sitting beside the bookcase where the school library was normally kept under lock and key.

She looked gorgeous and I stammered, "Hello."

She asked me to take down my trousers.

With shaky hands I unclipped the S-shaped buckle of my adjustable, three-colour elastic belt. Reaching out a hand, she began to feel my groin, counting two testicles present and correct. Then she asked me to take off my shirt and vest.

I wondered how far I'd have to go to prove everything I owned was in working order. Or if things went any further, would the other boys standing outside the door be able to hear us? She asked me to move closer. My eyes widened when she said I had to have a three-in-one vaccination and I spotted the needle. I seemed to be the only child in my class a week later that showed a reaction to a further jab she had given as a test for tuberculosis. And so my mother got an appointment card in the post, asking her to take me to the medical dispensary, a chilly out-house with a flat roof, built especially for the doctor to practice in our village. On a bright and carefree Saturday morning – not even a school morning – I had to abandon the outside world to sit in its waiting room.

Beside me sat a man with half his face disfigured by a blast in the mines, his scars irredeemably blue and black with fragments of slate and coal particles lodged there after the mis-timed explosion. He smiled when he caught me staring at his injury. He was a nice man but a frightening sight. Ahead of me sat a line of chesty coal-miners smoking unfiltered cigarettes, their fingers bronzed with nicotine.

The wire mesh used to reinforce the glass made the windows of the waiting room look frozen over. And the electric heater mounted on the wall overhead made no impression on the Siberian atmosphere. Sitting opposite the miners were elderly women dressed in winter coats and scarves, fur-lined boots and hats, making the place look and feel even more like the last outpost before the Gulag.

People coughed and shuffled their feet but traded few words. They were too busy listening for a door to open and, as the silence continued, wondering what sort of ailment might be keeping the person ahead of them so long with the doctor.

The last time I visited the doctor I had to swallow polio medicine soaked in a sugar cube. That was fine, since I had never before seen or tasted a sugar cube. And despite the grim atmosphere and the strong antiseptic smell that wafted from the inner surgery, when my turn came I walked manfully into the surgery and stood by the examination couch.

On my mother's instructions I took off my shirt and vest and prepared a smile to meet the lovely nurse again. The family doctor stepped out of the anteroom and left his stethoscope on my chest. The hands of death could not have felt any colder.

"Take a deep breath," Doctor Gibbons said. "Hold it. And let it out. Again."

As he listened to the rattle in my lungs, all I could think about was the mobile X-ray unit: a sinister looking Government Health Service van that stopped from time to time in the middle of our village. When it arrived, a queue of coal miners required to have a chest X-ray gathered by the van doors.

Being asthmatic and prone to chest infections my X-ray had been taken before. And I understood the compliant terror in which even grown men bared their chests for it. An icy metal plate located against the chest, followed by a quick intake and hold of breath. The burst of invisible X-rays, and then that negative image held up to the light to reveal an all clear or a spot on the lungs: the lethal shadow of coal dust or consumption that meant invalidity, slow suffocation and death.

As the doctor's stethoscope pressed against my bare flesh, I began to tremble uncontrollably. My heart raced so wildly I was convinced the doctor would tell my mother I needed a heart transplant. On every side of me I could see surgical instruments in stainless steel kidney-bowls, any one of which might be used next to operate on me. But I dared not whimper because of the slim thermometer wedged under my tongue. One wrong move and I could bite off the end and die of ground glass and mercury poisoning.

Doctor Gibbons nodded and began to prime a needle and syringe - a heavy glass-graduated syringe with a needle so big it would make you flinch if you saw it being used to inject cattle. And there seemed to be a load more needles exactly like it, rusting in the antique sterilising unit.

After a quick cool swab, the point of the needle pierced my arm and I stepped into a pool of smooth black quicksand. A high ringing note started in my ears and I woke up on the floor, with my whey-faced mother looking down at me, and the doctor shining a bright light in my eyes.

*

"Needles," I said to my mother, staring at the pile of syringes and needles that tumbled out of the packet from Aunt Teresa. "You know me and needles."

Worse followed. The 21-day course of injections was awaiting approval from the US Food and Drug Authority. And 714X wasn't even an orthodox medicine; it turned out to be a complementary treatment. "What are we going to do?" my mother asked, looking as horrified as I felt.

"We'll watch the video," I said.

The video presentation looked like an out-of-date Open University lecture. A clean-shaven man wearing a sports jacket said that a doctor who felt the key to human health was injecting essential elements into the lymph system had developed 714X. It employed a camphor suspension with elements injected directly into the large lymph node. This node could be found using the femoral artery as a starting point and then triangulating along a line from the groin to the navel. You then had to cool the exact spot with ice to prevent the camphor from evaporating while injecting precisely... On and on the man in the video went.

Hopeless, I thought. Hopeless, hopeless, hopeless.

It was a minute or more before we heard the phone on the hallway table ringing. I looked at my mother and she looked at me. I stopped the video.

"If that's Teresa," my mother said, "what will I tell her?"

"Do you want me to talk to her?"

"No," she said. "I'll get it."

She picked up the phone. "Hello."

I watched her nod her head sharply before she put her hand over the mouthpiece to tell me, "It's Lil. She's finished her radium treatment. She's back in the Regional Hospital for more tests but she's sitting up and walking again."

II

We got to the hospital before dinnertime. Lil sat propped up in bed but her eyes were closed. We stood at the foot of her bed, uncertain what to do. Every time Lil exhaled her short breaths rattled her lower lip, like an athlete pausing after a hectic sprint.

Ever since the doctor indicated to me it was only a matter of time for Lil I had hinted but never said directly to my mother that her illness was terminal. It felt unseemly and presumptuous to say categorically to my mother that her twin sister was going to die.

Lil stirred her head and perked up when she spotted us standing at her bedside. Awake, she looked much better than the last time we saw her. She said she was 'horrid weak'. But she had eaten a bit of porridge that morning and a slice of toast. She was in no pain, but she still had a mouth ulcer. Having the mouth ulcer made her wary of the seeds in the fig-rolls, but she liked a fig roll biscuit with her tea. And she had ordered mince and a spud for dinner. After that she thought she might have a spoonful of trifle.

To my mind, this was a huge improvement and I was glad now I'd downplayed the cemetery arithmetic. My mother, however, shifted uneasily. It was hard for her to accommodate her twin sister thinking in terms of the next hospital meal.

Both were great talkers however, and they were soon chatting over and across each other, juggling a load of topics, my mother saying how she read that Prince Andrew was starting in a new school in Scotland; Lil saying the girl who was supposed to tidy her hair hadn't appeared yet; my mother saying the cattle were fine and the red white-head cow was ready to calve. How would her son, Sean, manage? Lil wondered, adding she'd be happy to sit at home in her chair by the fire if she could bring a foot after her.

My mother mentioned the treatment that came in the post. Lil was supposed to have 21 injections over 21 days. She couldn't possibly give the injections to herself and we would have to ask the doctors or a nurse to administer them instead. Unfortunately, the medicine had no official approval in America or Europe. They might not want to give it to Lil.

Lil listened carefully, and then asked my mother, "What do you think?"

"Teresa has great faith in it," my mother said.

"But there's no saying what's in it," said Lil. "It might kill me."

While I had not told my mother outright what the doctor indicated to me, I was convinced my mother knew that her sister's time on earth might be short. But what about Lil? I wondered. Did she know for definite? She must know she was seriously ill. And her son and her daughters must also know. They might be better placed to guide her on this medication issue. Though the decision to undertake the course of injections or any other kind of therapy was finally for Lil alone.

Lil was my godmother and I liked to think we were close. But from the outset I had decided not to interfere in any decisions taken by Lil or her family in regard to her illness. If I had a role, it was to see that my mother had as much time as she wanted with her twin sister. And at that precise moment my mother looked relieved to hear Lil ruling out the injections.

I understood Lil's reluctance, but I wasn't sure we should dismiss the injection therapy outright. With cancer, or with any grave illness, you had to balance realism with hope. Teresa had gone to a lot of trouble to get hold of the treatment. She was a smart woman who honestly felt it would help. And it was human nature to believe in alternative remedies. Lil's situation was extreme. But I knew what it felt like to be sick and afraid. As a child I had asthma. Bad asthma. When the relentless coughing fits started, my mother had to hold me while I hung out an open window, blue in the face, and frantic to catch the next breath of air.

In between the asthma attacks my mother deployed a barrage of home remedies to keep me alive and breathing. Every morning she dosed me with a spoonful of cod-liver oil before going to school. She followed the cod liver oil with an even more disgusting spoonful of malt extract. The taste and smell of both repeated in my mouth all day. There were also evil-smelling dilutions of TCP for sore throats and generous smears of Vic's ointment rubbed into the hollow of my chest for wheezing fits. The phrase *Doctor Gibbons says* was used to sanction all kinds of treatments outside that kindly man's more orthodox efforts to improve my health in his medical dispensary. Doctor Gibbons says, "You have to wear a vest". Doctor

Gibbons says, "You shouldn't be out at night in the frost playing football". Doctor Gibbons says, "You shouldn't come home in a sweat. And too much television is bad for your eyes."

Along with medicines off the shelf, my mother and her sister shared a miniature bottle of olive oil. After warming the oil, they poured it into our ears, using a cotton wool plug to cure me, my brothers and our cousins, all of us prone to earache. A damp flannel left on the forehead was used to bring down a temperature. Suck on a clove for a toothache. Nettle stings got a rub from a dock leaf. Cuts were scalded with liquid iodine and bandaged with strips torn from cotton bed sheets retired from use to the back of the hot-press. A dash of whiskey went into a mug with a raw egg whisked through warm milk and a spoon of sugar as a tonic or to help us sleep. A red flannel band was reserved for a chill on the kidneys. I got a hot-water bottle and an Aspro tablet for the common cold, supplemented by a large bottle of Lucozade and thick arrowroot biscuits for a bout of influenza. On bright summer evenings my mother hung a blanket outside my bedroom window to convince me it was dark outside and time to go to sleep.

When it came to a serious illness my mother relied on her holy relic: a smidgen of red fabric in a reliquary the size of an overcoat button. She trusted in this relic the way other people believed in the phenomenal properties of penicillin.

The time I got sick with a terrible drowsiness and a headache so bad even dim light hurt my eyes she applied the relic. For two days I drifted in and out of consciousness. I was burning up with a temperature and I had all the major symptoms of meningitis. But she insisted it was migraine and sat praying over me, holding a damp flannel on my forehead, with the holy relic pinned to the lapel of my pyjamas. On the third day I came around and asked her to open the bedroom curtains. Again I saw my mother looking down at me with a pale face while a bright light shone in my eyes.

I survived into adulthood and the asthma abated. But the experience taught me that above and beyond the home remedies it was love that kept me alive. The love of my mother for the children she brought into the world and cherished through every upset and illness. It was love that made Teresa in America press upon Nan and Lil this terrifying course of injections. And it was the love these twin sisters had for each other that would point the way forward, as I attended again to their conversation which had turned to Teresa.

"I had a phone call from America," my mother told Lil. "Teresa is coming home on holiday."

"Is she staying long?" Lil asked.

"Two weeks."

"It's a lot of trouble for you," said Lil. "Where will you put her?"

"In the big room. I'll have to replace the wallpaper."

Lil nodded.

The girl arrived with the dinner trolley. We pulled back our seats to make room.

The girl lifted the stainless-steel cover from the plate and handed across a serving of mashed potato and warm minced beef in gravy.

"That looks nice," my mother said.

"They have me on morphine," Lil said. "And sometimes my stomach feels sick. But I thought I'd try a bit of mince."

At the mention of morphine my mother glanced across at me. We said nothing, but we should have realised the mixed bouts of sleep and elation were the result of the drug.

I put the dinner on the table in front of Lil and she took up a fork. Now that we were on our feet we felt we should leave Lil alone to eat in comfort. Before we left, we plumped up her pillows, fixed her bib and made sure she had her trifle as well as a glass of milk near at hand and a drink of 7-Up.

"Your appetite is good," my mother said.

"I need to keep up me strength," Lil said.

Lil had an unspoken conviction that as long as she could eat she might still be coming home. She linked appetite with strength and strength with survival. And even though she was on morphine it was good to see her so positive.

As we prepared to leave, my mother gave Lil a pat on the head and whispered, "God love you."

Lil looked up from her dinner at my mother and said, "It's you I'm worried about."

III

Getting the home place ready for Teresa to stay was the next assignment. I thought the house and sheds and my mother's garden looked fine. My mother had different ideas. To get ready for Teresa, she said, meant a list of jobs as long as her arm. I said nothing. Getting the home place ready for the American visitors was a tradition that went back as far as I could remember.

Every few years a tissue-thin airmail letter with candy-striped borders arrived from the United States. Before my mother had the last sentence of the letter read she was in a state. Her family, she said, were coming "home on holiday". Every inch of the home place would have to be painted or wallpapered, the barns whitewashed, the lane repaired, the hedges cut and boiling water put out to kill the weeds in the yard.

In the weeks that followed, the stairs and skirting and ceiling boards all got a dollop of oak-brown, larkspur-blue or white hard-gloss paint. Even the table and the kitchen chairs were freshly painted and left out in the yard to dry. "I'm run stupid," my mother said, when anyone asked how things were going.

Calm descended only late at night. Then we took out the family photo album with the cardboard covers done like tooled leather. The album had stiff oblong pages made from black sugar-paper with tiny slits and white brackets to secure the photographs. But the whole thing had to be picked up and kept horizontal or the loose photos and mementoes would spill out: black and white snapshots and Eastman Kodak Company colour photographs with the magenta cast of a hot climate. Polaroid and Instamatic snaps. Studio portraits. All gathered loosely between the pages of a photo album with the quality of memory, a hodgepodge of pictures, imprecise dates and overlaps where people, places and events merged out of sequence: Ozone Park, Labour Day, 1964. Rockaway, 23rd of August 1957. Jones Beach. 1961. Long Island, 1967. The World Fair.

Preserved between the black sugar-paper pages of the same album were the Cunard shipping line menus and postcards written during the initial crossing from Ireland to America. Evidence of the first exotic rewards of travel. Proofs of the small luxuries tasted.

A highlight amongst the early photographs was a picture of Nan and Lil's older sister, Teresa, at a formal Irish-American dinner. Teresa's smile and fresh complexion revealed a girl barely out of her teens. She wore her best dress and her smile gleamed like the silverware ranged in orderly settings the length of the table. It might have been a society wedding, a social banquet, a Saint Patrick's Day dinner, a Thanksgiving or an Independence Day celebration. Even more glorious than the setting was the expression on Teresa's face, the look in her eyes, so dazzled and so proud. The total astonishment at the way her life had been transformed.

All our relations in America looked prosperous in the photographs; the women with their matching shoes and handbags, dressed in the style of Grace Kelly and Jackie Kennedy. The men in sharp suits opening presents with their children under enormous and lavishly decorated Christmas trees in plush suburban homes on Long Island, in Chicago, Boston, Connecticut, Washington and Philadelphia.

They looked happy and content. But in the wake of President John F. Kennedy's visit to Ireland, a powerful strain of homesickness overtook the Irish community in America. Kennedy's visit evoked a fierce pride in Irish roots and an intense nostalgia for the old country. In their mind's eye, many Irish Americans began to imagine the golden barley-straw thatched roofs and whitewashed walls and little cottages set among 40 shades of green fields - a dream of Ireland suddenly more alluring than all the bounty of America. The advent of charter flights made a two-week visit to Ireland possible and they came looking for that misty-eyed vision with the help of the mighty dollar.

For practical purposes many had become full American citizens over the years and pledged their allegiance to the Stars and Stripes. Their passports were blue with an American bald eagle crest on the front cover. Their children were tanned and blonde, and most wore dental braces fitted by the family orthodontist. They believed themselves to be Irish, not just Irish at heart, but Irish by right of birth. Yet their accents were American. Their children were American. And no one wanted them to be subtle or soft-spoken. They were supposed to be glamorous and brash and better off: the kind of people portrayed in the photographs. When they left home they were Irish, but we greeted their return with a single phrase - "The Yanks are landed."

On the day the Americans were expected we kept looking towards the end of the lane, maintaining a tight watch until the gate next to the road swung open. When the hired car nosed through, we roared, "The Yanks are landed."

"Hush," my mother said taking off her housecoat. .

We met our visitors at the front door, and from the moment the Americans carried their huge suitcases into the house all normal activity stopped. We downed tools on the farm and chores were cut back to the minimum.

Even my mother's scant cosmetics, her make-up, hair-rollers, eye lotion, jar of Pond's cold cream and the bottle of Glycerine she used to smooth her work-chapped hands faded out of sight. Exotic suntan and moisturising creams, lotions and cleansers, and strange tasting American tooth gel and reels of impossible to use dental floss invaded the bathroom. There were men's wash bags and shaving kits and a powerful whiff of Old Spice after-shave. An electric razor with an adapter to lower the voltage took over the window ledge. The shelves filled up with medicine bottles for dodgy stomachs and constipation. The Americans even had a first-aid kit that had us hope for a small cut on a finger so we could try out the spotlessly clean Band-Aid sticking plasters.

Once they settled in, we had to keep the coal fire revved up all day, because the American's were "perished to the bone" by the damp Irish climate. The visitors were all morning in the bathroom and despite our best efforts they ran so much hot water the pipes constantly air-locked.

Our cousins didn't like the "bugs" – the moths and daddy-long-legs – that flew around the light bulbs at night because our home had no window screens. But if the children were boisterous and demanding, their parents made generous presents to my mother, of bath towels and American bed linen that she considered the finest in the world.

We never gave much thought to the lives of our American aunts and uncles, nieces, nephews and cousins; their marriages, their jobs or the neighbourhoods where they lived and worked and saved so hard for these precious trips back to the old country. To our minds they were magically prosperous. They dismissed every expenditure saying, "What's a couple of bucks?!"

We knew nothing about their early lives, except what we could guess from the photographs taken in Ireland before they left. These photographs were smaller than the American snapshots and taken in black and white. A parting record of young lads and girls with wry smiles back then, dressed in their Sunday best as they stood in front of stone-built cottages and homesteads. Quiet but determined. They had the look of voyagers with one eye already on the raised torch of Lady Liberty.

Once they reached America they sent home beguiling portraits of the good life on the other side of the Atlantic. They longed for their brothers and sisters to join them. They wanted to look after their own. But not everyone could emigrate.

Ireland meant home. But what good was a home if no one lived there? Somebody had to stay and look after the home place. It was uncomfortable to think of a mother and father and brothers and sisters living in poverty. But as long as they had relatives in Ireland the ones who went to America would never feel totally uprooted. They would have that living connection with the place where they were born and reared, even if the people there would never be well off, would always be the poor relations. And so their lives abroad in America were steeped in these contradictory emotions. Those deep bonds of love and guilt, prosperity and liability epitomised by the amount of dollars constantly sent back to Ireland.

They kept up that image of prosperity whenever they came home on holiday. On every trip there had to be one big shopping expedition. When they got back from town, the Americans always had some improvement for the house: a roll of carpet for the middle of the stairs or a towel-rail for the bathroom. The metal meat-safe with the tiny ventilation holes in the sides got ousted from the scullery by a new white fridge with a freezer compartment on top and a plastic tray for making ice cubes.

My mother appreciated and accepted the generosity of her visitors, but not all of the changes sat easily with her. There was the implication that after all the hard work, the cleaning and the cooking, her homemaking wasn't good enough, or could be improved.

We children were blind to these underlying tensions. As long as the Americans occupied our house, we wanted only that happy, expansive atmosphere. But the bubble burst when the Americans set the wind-up alarm clock to go off at five in the morning for the drive back to Shannon Airport.

Before they left they fought the battle of the bulge with a platoon of plaid suitcases packed with souvenirs from home: Waterford Crystal,

Galtee sausages and bacon, Calvita processed cheese, Irish linen, Cadbury's Dairy Milk and Fry's Cream Chocolate, white woollen Aran sweaters, tea towels printed with corny proverbs and recipes for Irish Coffee and Irish Stew, the likes of which we'd never tasted.

When we were younger we waved the Americans off standing in a bunch at our front door. In later years we went with them to the airport. And the whole business of seeing the Americans off at the airport heightened the contrast between our lives and theirs.

Nobody in our house had a passport. Just to be an airline passenger seemed an extraordinary privilege. Our definition of extravagance was having money to spend in the duty free goods shop. The green shamrock livery of Aer Lingus we thought the height of special treatment and luxury.

There was also the glamorous legacy of the flying boats that once set down on the Shannon estuary at Foynes. Not to mention the aura of fame provided by the film stars and celebrities who stopped at Shannon over the years, to be photographed waving from the open passenger doors of twin propeller Douglas DC-3s and Lockheed Constellations. Every girl wanted to be an air hostess. The pilots in their uniforms, walking towards the aircraft they captained, were even more cool, calm and collected than Steve Silvermint.

It broke our hearts when the final boarding call came. The Irish coffees were drained. Our cousins cried. The adults hugged. The departures gate closed. For as long as the Americans were home on holiday we were on holiday in our own home. Then the plane took off and all of us had to go back to our workaday lives.

IV

The lane into Lil's house curved through pasture fields and mixed properties. Two sets of farm gates belonging to different owners had to be opened and closed to make headway. I would forever associate visits to my Aunt Lil's house with getting in and out of the car to open and close gates.

Though they lived in practically identical farmhouses the atmosphere around Lil's house was very different to my mother's home place. My mother lived on the side of the mountain. One by one the population had thinned out around her and the lights of her neighbours had disappeared. But she still had people passing on the road and calling around the house. Lil's house was more fiercely isolated.

It stood a long way in from the road. On each side of the winding lane into the house, cattle stood bunched together in the pasture, enduring the sleet and rain while wintering out, or laying down next the lane in the summer, chewing the cud in field upon field of daisies and clover, thistle and ragwort. In the spring the rushes growing on the hills overlooking the lane had to be cut. In the winter the drains had to be cleaned. Or as Lil once described it, "Cutting sprat all summer and turning daub all winter."

The small lake neighbouring Lil's house was fringed with rowan trees, and shimmering rows of silver birch trees stretched further into the bog.

While the lake supported coarse fish, pike and perch and bream, this isolated terrain was itself a stronghold for native wildlife: rabbit, hare, fox, badger, pine martin, otter and lately mink. Hen and cock pheasants strolled the lane unhindered; plump woodpigeon cooed in the ivy-covered bushes; speckled thrush sang in the tree crowns; sparrows, finches, fiery breasted robins and bright-beaked blackbirds lorded over the whitethorn hedges and the scented gorse bushes; the cuckoo announced the spring and the corncrake until recently carried on into the summer. Woodpeckers tapped like magical shoe-menders in thickets of hazel and pine and blackthorn. Yellowhammers waited for the crop of oats and crows attacked the autumn apples. On frosty winter nights the migrant Hooper Swans honked and crossed in silhouette under the stars. And winging closer to the ground in total silence, only to put the heart crossways with its banshee screech, the white barn owl, its unearthly cry matched only by the blood curdling yelps of a roving fox in heat in the winter fields cracking with frost. And in the midst of this remoteness stood Lil's two-storey family farmhouse with outlying buildings and machinery and cattle in the fields, a testament to hard endeavour on the margins.

When we pulled up in front of the house I spotted Lil. She was in her familiar seat at the kitchen table with her back to the television. She turned her head to look out the window into the lane to see whose car had arrived. On seeing her I felt a sudden tightness in my throat, and getting out of the car I thought how this wilderness would endure, with or without this farmhouse, and the woman who kept the place immaculate. But it would never have the same meaning again without this woman at the heart of it all.

To everyone's surprise, Lil was out of the hospital and home again. We did not know for how long. But she had made it home and that was the important thing. From the updates given to me by my mother I knew that Lil's daughter, Geraldine, was flying in from America for two weeks. Her daughter Maeve had already been over from England to see Lil. Maeve had to get back. But Lil's son Sean was living at home and he was there night and day to look after his mother. She also had supporting visits from the physiotherapist and the Public Health Nurse, and an application had been made for home help.

I drove around by the side of house to find a turning place for the car. Sean was outside, dressed in overalls and working on his own car. He'd grown out of the boy-racer stage, but he still had a fondness for cars.

My mother said hello to Sean and went into the house to see Lil. I held back to have a word with Sean. I hadn't really talked to him about his mother and he hadn't talked to me. I wanted to give him an opening.

He asked me about the car I was driving. I told him it was going well, "touch wood". There had been another accident at Greyfield Bridge, he said. He'd just got back with the tractor after pulling the driver's car out of the ditch.

Greyfield Bridge was an accident black-spot. Speeding cars were always taking the turn too fast at the old-fashioned cut stone bridge. It happened so often that the man living nearest the bridge, Henry Daly could tell by the sound of a car engine as it raced by the house if the driver would successfully navigate the turn or not. On nights when he heard a car zoom past too fast he would put on his coat, find his flashlight, and start walking towards the bridge, even as it dawned on the driver that they had run out of road.

Sean told me he was visiting Henry Daly the other night when a car raced by. Henry got his coat and lamp and Sean went with him. They found a metallic-blue Honda Civic lying on one side in the field below the bridge. The passenger door was open but the driver was still inside fumbling in the dark.

"Shine that light down here," he called from the wreck.

"Is your leg trapped?" Sean asked.

"I'm fine," the driver said. "But I have a bottle of vodka down here somewhere and I think it's broken."

We left off telling stories and I walked with Sean towards the house. Beside the back door I spotted Lil's pushbike. Anyone who knew Lil had a fixed image of this spare, hardy and self-reliant countrywoman in a raincoat and headscarf with a bag of shopping hung on the handlebars of her bicycle, weathering the country roads and refusing all offers of a lift. We passed the bicycle without making any remarks.

The kettle steamed on the hob of the cream Rayburn. Working clothes and wool socks hung to dry on the rail above the fire. With the stove lit, the kettle steaming and the clothes drying, the kitchen had a cosy and permanent feeling. The stay in hospital might never have happened.

Lil sat talking cheerfully to my mother, telling her how good she felt. Though not as good as she was a month ago when she was still able to cycle every day to her part-time job picking mushrooms, or to O'Donnell's shop in the village to collect her usual order, or pay what she owed in the book at the end of the week.

Sean said the authorities were widening the road and replacing the original stone bridge at Greyfield with a new concrete job.

"I don't know how many times I cycled over that bridge and back," said Lil. "'Twas my life, all told."

Lil was amongst the last of a particular breed of countrywomen and men on their 'high Nelly' bicycles with a bag for shopping or a coat tied in a bundler on the back carrier going about their business steadfast and independent.

Like my father, Lil's husband John Beirne never learned how to drive and never owned a car. Motorcars were costly and both households lacked money. But I had the impression that my father and John Beirne never rated car ownership the priority other men did. They seemed to believe that if they found their true direction in life the cars, the money and the rewards would follow. They were not betting men, but they were both gamblers.

For Lil's husband John, his gamble was politics.

John never missed a party meeting or a rally. He was always there to take up church gate collections. He got hot under the collar when arguments started along party lines. He put more time and energy into politics than he put into farming. And when a close friend went forward as a candidate in the local elections, John became an enthusiastic campaigner.

Shortly before the election a dispute broke out between the opposing factions. In the heat of the argument, John called one of the rival candidates a mug.

"Define a mug for me?" the candidate asked John.

John said, "A mug is a man with neither balls nor brains."

Who knows how far it might have taken John from his remote farm if the voting had gone a different way. But John was left out of pocket and out of power when the mug won the election.

You gamble, you lose, and you live with the consequences. And I had not come that day to dwell on the past. What man or woman hasn't taken a chance in life that failed to pay a dividend? But I couldn't help thinking that if my father and John Beirne had gambled and lost, it was the women they married who paid the higher price.

"I hope you're not over doing it," my mother said, looking at a basin full of potato skins on the table in front of Lil.

For the first time I noticed that Lil was dressed in an old skirt, a collarless top and a cardigan with a thin belt around the waist. That is, the outfit she used working around the house.

"I was getting a bit of dinner for Sean," she said.

"I keep telling her there's no need," Sean said, pacing over and back in front of the fireplace.

We understood Sean did not want Lil making a fuss, cooking and tidying up and trying to look after him and the housework. But it was Lil's way of keeping going. And we couldn't condemn her for wanting to feel useful.

Oprah was on the television behind Lil's back, engaged in one of her motivational self-help chats about the higher qualities in life. The terms used were pleasure, meaning, and wholeness. There was no mention of selflessness. But for Lil and my mother the highest quality in life was giving - even if giving meant that tenderness was often expressed as fretfulness, intimacy as constant worry and love as total sacrifice.

"Did you hear from Teresa?" Lil asked.

"She's arriving in a fortnight's time," my mother said.

"I don't want her coming all this way just to see me," Lil said, twisting the tea towel in her fist into a tight bind.

"She was coming home on holiday anyway," my mother bluffed

"We'll never have this place ready in time," Lil said, looking to Sean.

"What were you thinking of doing?" my mother shot a worried glance at Sean.

"The windows need replacing," he said.

"Could it not wait?" I said.

"The window in the front room is falling asunder," he said.

"Can I take a look?" I said. We went into the front room together: a farmhouse parlour with a fusty unused air. The room looked big and cold with the furniture in disarray and the curtains off the window.

"The wind is whistling in the gaps," Sean said pressing his thumb into the window sash until moisture sprang from the spongy timber. "The whole lot will have to be replaced," he said, "upstairs and down."

I wanted to tell him that his time might be better spent with his mother. In a couple of weeks she might not be as good as she was now: on her feet, lucid, alive.

I lowered my voice and asked, "Did you talk to the doctors?"

"I know the situation," he said.

"You're going to have a lot on your hands, Sean."

"It'll only take a week or so," he said. "And my mother will be glad next winter when she finds the heat they keep in."

Though we were standing in the same room, our eyes beheld different prospects. I saw only the place turned inside-out. But Sean's eyes were fixed on the end result: a cosy, refurbished room where his mother could convalesce.

Lil had left the kitchen and come into the hallway with my mother.

On her feet, she looked stooped and frail. She could hobble only with the aid of a walking stick and she fared slowly along the tiled floor.

"How are you managing the stairs, Lil?" my mother asked.

"I'm working it," Lil said.

"She's afraid a bone in her back is going to snap," Sean said shaking his head in exasperation, "and she's still trying to climb stairs."

"I have an appointment in two weeks for a calcium boost," Lil said with a colour rising in her pale cheeks. "And Sean is going to fit a handrail for me."

"You were advised not to use the stairs," Sean said.

"Then we'll move the bed downstairs," Lil said.

Without consultation I said, "You could always stay with my mother for a while. At least while the windows are going in."

"I'm grand where I am," Lil said.

She hobbled towards the front door; she opened it and said, "I should have offered ye a cup of tea?"

"Don't go making tea," my mother said. "Rest yourself and we'll call again."

We had not intended to leave so soon, but Lil was already engaged in the motions of seeing us off. "I don't know what I was thinking," she said. "These tablets have me confused."

But Lil was not the least bit confused. And she had no notion of making tea. It was suddenly clear to me I had made a huge blunder. Lil was afraid. No, Lil was terrified. Terrified that we wanted her out of her house. She was prepared to sleep upstairs or downstairs, in her usual chair in the kitchen or a cubby hole under the stairs if necessary - as long as she could stay in her own house. Having made it out of the hospital she was determined not to stop in the half-way house of her twin sister; the house where she was born and grew up. She wanted her independence. She wanted her separate identity. She wanted to be at home.

"Are you sure you'll be okay?" my mother said in parting.

And Lil said, "I'll take my chances here."

HIGHER POWERS

THURSDAY'S CHILD

Mammy had left us. I got back from school with my brother, Terry, and found only our dog, Harvey, inside the front door minding an empty bungalow in Arigna. Terry went from room to room, and finding nobody at home he got it into his head Mammy had left us for certain. She was gone and she was never coming back.

"Why?" I asked.

"Because Daddy has no job and we're not wanted here any longer," he said, before he ran from the house, bawling his eyes out.

I was nine years old and determined to keep a level head. The cream Rayburn was lit but damped down. I took the ashtray outside, loaded more coal on the fire and turned up the draft. When I had the fire going strong I put a saucepan of milk on the hot plate to warm. Then I got the loaf of white sliced bread from the cupboard and loaded the sugar bowl.

The front door opened and my younger brother, who had been off school for a couple of days with an earache, came in ahead of my mother. She had bundled him into a warm coat with the hood up and taken him with her to visit her mother and father on the farm on the mountain.

But now she got a shock when she found we had made it home from school before she got back.

"I'm so sorry," she said.

Seeing her again hit me with greater force than the thought that she had gone and left us forever. I felt my lower lip quiver, but I tugged hard at my earlobe and kept my feelings to myself.

Spotting the loaf bread and the saucepan of milk set to warm, she asked me what I had in mind. Reluctantly, I confessed that I was making "goodie".

"Were you not worried," she asked, "when you found no one at home?"

"If you didn't come back we'd have to get along without you," I said, patting Harvey on the head.

She stood watching me closely, but Terry, who was still wandering around outside and bawling, broke the silence. She went out to find and comfort him. I passed Harvey his share of the warm milk and bread sops doused with sugar.

When Terry and Mammy got back, I had my shoes off and my feet warming on the hob. Nourished by the "goodie" I felt settled, even reassured that in the worst of circumstances I had kept the household going and proved myself wiser than my older brother.

My mother continued to stand in the middle of the kitchen floor, stroking the hair on Terry's head.

"I've been to see Granny and Grandad," she said. "And we're moving in with them."

"Why?" I cried, though she did not have to put forth a reason.

A HUMBLE ACCOUNT

When my mother moved with her family back to the farmhouse where she was reared, she found the place riddled with woodworm. "Every stick of furniture had to be replaced." But Matt was out of work and the farm was in debt and she couldn't afford to buy new furniture outright in one payment. The neighbours said she should talk to Paddy Smith.

Paddy had broad shoulders and a mellow voice and he acted as an agent for Sloanes of Sligo. He wore a tweed cap and a gabardine raincoat with a bundle of accounts like a brick in his inside pocket.

He told Nan he could bring her whatever she wanted, from a wind-up alarm clock to a nest of tables, from a bedside locker to a fold-out settee, from a wardrobe to a matching pair of flannelette sheets or a candlewick bedspread. All at a good price, but with added interest of course.

To help her children settle into the upstairs bedroom allotted to us she ordered new beds, with a spring mattress for me to replace the original 'horsehair' fibre mattress that aggravated my asthma. After the first down-payment, Paddy called each week. Nan always invited him into the kitchen, but he never sat down. He preferred to hover. When she offered him tea, he said he'd take "a drop in his hand". He drank his cup of tea standing up, while she found the pound note, or if money happened to be tight that week, the ten-shilling note, put aside in advance and kept between the pages of her book.

"Anything at all," Paddy said, accepting the smallest amount, "to write in the book."

Then he opened her book and he wrote in the payment and the date before he folded away the money. He understood his clients and payments were clearly recorded in full sight.

The additional interest charged might be high, but every

instalment brought her a little bit closer to the point where she hoped Paddy would not consider it unseemly if she put in another order and raised the bill again. For her next order she had him bring a two-bar electric heater, and we stood in the glow of its toasty warmth whenever we undressed at bedtime in our chill upstairs room.

Along with household goods and furniture, Paddy Smith sold clothes. Most of the young lads around home bought their suits on hire purchase from Paddy. But the single men weren't nearly as reliable as the housewives. The first payment was often the last payment when the new suit was bought only for the client to take the boat to England.

Others wore the new suits to a dance in the Mayflower Ballroom in Drumshanbo or the Ballroom of Romance in Glenfarne, where it was an important part of any good night out to redden your knuckles in a brawl with the first man who looked at you the wrong way. Still others had standing feuds to settle behind the marquee at the Black Spot carnival in Leitrim. Whatever the cause of the row, some man was bound to come home with the good suit in tatters, the seams burst, a lapel or a sleeve missing.

Another client would have a spill off his Honda 50 coming home from the pub full of pints, leaving the bike up to the maker's nameplate in the ditch and the backside torn out of the new suit.

Then came the quiet knock. And the smallest and most innocent-looking child got the job of opening the front door.

"Is your brother at home?" Paddy enquired with a glance over the child's head into the kitchen.

"He's out. He's gone to the pub."

"Tell him he forgot to bring his legs."

The feet under the kitchen table were pulled back in a hurry. Whether he got paid or not, Paddy never made a fuss. He called the next week and the week after and the week after that with the patience that gets a snail to Jerusalem.

Paddy never tired, but in the long run his clients got fed up paying the high interest rates and being so beholden to one man and one outlet. Sloanes' business arrangements began to resemble a vintage car, impressive but antiquated, left behind by the size and power of the new chain-stores and the more nifty ladies fashion boutiques and dedicated men's shops.

"They did us no favours, but I was sorry to see them go," my mother said when Paddy stopped calling with goods from Sloanes. Nearly everybody had an article bought on the hire purchase at one time or another. And the whole road used to look forward to a visit from the delivery van, even if Paddy Smith and his long account books followed in its shadow. He remained a welcome figure in the lives of my mother and her sister Lil and a whole generation of house-proud women on small incomes at the centre of a world that revolved around hire purchase. Patient but determined women who steadily modernised the country by weekly instalments.

HIGHER POWERS

Crosshill was the name of the farm on the mountain. And during the month of May I roved around Crosshill, gathering wild flowers every morning before going to school. The flowers went into a jam jar full of water kept at the foot of a plaster statue of the Blessed Virgin in my bedroom upstairs. The lady-delicate fragrance of the primroses, gathered on May mornings with the dewdrops on their petals became inseparable from my idea of the mother of God, her beauty, goodness and mercy.

The quick green buds on the trees breaking into summer leaf, the mantillas of white blossom on the hawthorns, and the wild woods brimming with bluebells, woodruff and eyebright were so beautiful they could only be the handiwork of an all powerful Creator. As I wandered in search of fresh flowers every morning, my Wellington boots made the first path in the dew-drenched fields and I imagined the path to heaven must shine just as bright.

In the middle room of our three-classroom school I was also being prepared for my first Holy Communion. Sickness meant that my school attendance was poor and I had been held back, making me older than the average age of the Communion class. Even though I tried very hard I was too much the solitary daydreamer to be a good scholar. And I found the formal prayers awkward and confusing. "The fruit of thy womb, Jesus" - I had no idea what that meant.

After weeks of preparation, we arrived at the chapel in Arigna to practice our First Confession. Waiting my turn, I sat on a long wooden seat at the back of the chapel, fidgeting with the rest of the young Communion class. The dimly lit church smelled nothing like primroses. Dry boards creaked. The statues looked eerie. And I could hear no birdsong, only whispers and hollow echoes.

An elbow prodded me in the ribs and I got up and walked to the confession box. Opening the door, I stepped inside and the door closed behind me. I was unnerved by the airless gloom inside the confession box. I could hear voices but I didn't know if I should wait, or if the priest was sitting in the dark braced for my sins.

The hatch above the kneeler didn't appear to be open, but if it was, it meant a hard-working God with an entire Universe to run was waiting for me to begin. I began to babble my prayers.

Several minutes later the hatch on my side banged open. I got such a hop the prayers dried on my tongue. Not just the Confiteor - I forget every prayer I ever knew. Even the words, "Bless me, Father, for I have sinned." I could clearly see the annoyance on the priest's face behind the grill. And with no words or prayer forthcoming, he hounded me out of the confession box.

The next morning the priest came to our school. We stood up behind our desks when he walked into the classroom. I felt nervous but enormously relieved. I had one last chance to get my confession right and the priest had come to iron out the flaws. He leaned in close to the teacher and whispered in her ear. Her face stiffened.

She looked at each of us in turn. Her eyes came to me, stopped, and moved on.

The priest left and nothing was said until the end of the day when the teacher asked me to stay back after school. It came as a great relief that the teacher had not singled me out before the whole class and instead given me the chance to explain what happened in private.

Punishment was swift and painful.

In religion class we had been told you could confess to murder and if you were truly sorry and pleaded for forgiveness the priest could tell no one, not even the police. The seal of the confessional was absolute and unbreakable. A priest had to offer you God's grace and at worst inflict a heavy penance – ten Hail Marys or more maybe. But with each airy swish of the cane the pain that exploded from the tender palms of my hands seared a message into my brain: God's work might be everywhere in nature, but the teachings in my classroom and the promises made by the church were transparently man-made. A wise man lived with his sins and trusted no higher power.

VISITORS

It fell to me to get my father. We had visitors coming for the evening tea and he was in the pub. I did not want to go. My father never once lifted an angry hand to my two brothers or to me but he drank too much. My mother said so. My grandmother clucked her tongue. My grandfather had nothing to add.

Though the colliery owners no longer employed my father as a gardener because of ill health, he was now labouring seven days a week on my grandparents' farm on the mountain. Most evenings he went to the pub to meet the coal-miners after work.

The walk to the pub in the village took me down from the mountain. At the crossroads for the valley I chose the shortcut, a by-road known as the Horseshoe. People said the Horseshoe was one of the original pilgrim roads walked by Saint Patrick. Now the Horseshoe had a line of planks at one point, used to cross a hollow that was a parched dustbowl after a dry spell, but which flooded after heavy rain.

The pub was next door to the shop and petrol pump facing the field where Saint Ronan's football club were training. Although it was early in the evening several cars were parked haphazardly in front of the pub: a Volkswagen beetle, a Ford Cortina and a Vauxhall Viva. Amongst them stood the tractors with transport boxes loaded with coal and briquettes, the engine left running on one tractor with no battery. Honda 50 motorbikes were risen up on their centre stands; one with a cracked windshield and a white carrier box with blue baler twine holding the lid in place. Another had fertilizer bags fixed to the front as leg shields. A man's bicycle with a pump under the cross bar leaned against the wall, a bundle of oilskins strapped to the carrier, and a sheepdog asleep beside the back wheel. My father, like me, had walked to the pub.

Inside the front porch of the pub I encountered two brown

wooded doors. The door to the right opened into a new 'Singing Lounge' with a long flat roof and coloured bulbs along the eaves. It was mobbed on Sunday nights but rarely used during the week. The door on the left had a stick-on black plaque with gold lettering saying Bar. Every fibre in my body tightened opening that door.

There was a short leatherette-covered seat under the bar window but the coal-miners were gathered along the bar on high stools. Our dog, Harvey, lay under the bench seat by the window. My father was at the bar, drinking with the Man from Atlantis. A name earned after the man walked into the river one evening on his way home from the pub. When his sister was told her bachelor brother was in the river she replied, 'That's the place for him.'

The coal-miners were in their working clothes and my father wore his usual leather boots with the tops of his socks outside his trousers, and a trademark black beret pushed back on his head. The top buttons of his shirt were undone, showing a sunburnt neckline and a white vest inside his plaid working shirt. He held his cigarette cupped in the palm of his hand, as if keeping it safe from a spring breeze.

When he spotted me he said, "How is the cat jumping?"

"Mammy is looking for you," I said.

I was given a glass of red lemonade and a bag of crisps, but could not enjoy this sudden treat. At that moment I felt closer to our dog, Harvey, loyally waiting under the seat for my father, but also ready to let out a heavy sigh each time fresh pints were ordered. And every time the dog gave a sigh, I went forward again to remind him that Mammy was looking for him; that his tea was ready, that we all wanted him to come home.

The longer I sat there, the more I wondered why my mother hadn't come to fetch him, instead sending a child in her place.

Finally, finishing his drink, he turned to me and said, "We'll dab."

One of the younger coal-miners at the bar gave us a lift home in his Volkswagen Beetle. I sat quietly in the back with Harvey on my lap, listening to the air whistle and throb after my father opened the front passenger window to toss away the end of his cigarette. When we got out at the road gate, Harvey sprang from the car and ran on ahead down the lane to announce our return.

*

Dressed to meet the visitors in a wool-blend sports jacket, pressed trousers and heavy rimmed glasses, my father looked like a man just back from the office. But he found himself shut out from approval in this sober company around the supper table.

The sliced ham and tomatoes, lettuce and fresh scallions were shared around. And I found myself watching my father trying to appear at ease as he munched his food and looked about the table, nodding whenever anyone spoke. An effort that was doomed the moment he reached for the bottle of Chef brown sauce. The cap sprang off as he picked up the bottle, but he never noticed and he kept twisting the glass neck, thinking the cap wouldn't budge. My mother, Granny and Grandad, and our visitors all pretended not to notice, but I felt I had to point out to him that the cap from the sauce bottle was already on the floor.

At the first opportunity I left the table. I didn't want to stick around and I had in mind a long walk with Harvey in the twilight, not telling anyone where I was going. When we first moved to Crosshill I used to creep out of our room at night and cross the landing to listen at the newel post to the adults down below. Now I was glad to go walking.

There had been a time if I got scolded or upset by a row in the house, I would go off in a sulk and hide up a tree. High above the world in the cover of mottled sycamore leaves, I took guilty pleasure hearing my mother's anxious voice calling out my name, as the dusk fell and an ache grew in the pit of my stomach. That'll teach them, I thought. They'll miss me and they'll be sorry. And I imagined what it would be like if I stayed hidden until officially presumed dead, and my mother and father wound up holding hands, standing over a white coffin.

Outside the front door of the farmhouse, a waist high wall separated the cement-paved area we called the front street from the lawn and the flower garden. The cement street and the wall were warm after the hot day. We had enjoyed several hot days in a row, but the air was now humid and still and I got the feeling of rain on the way.

My skin began to tingle and when I looked at the front of my shirt I found it crawling with ants. I noticed then that the top of the wall around the front street was swarming with pismires. Flying pismires. Multitudes of familiar red ants and bigger black ants had sprouted wings and arrived at our house flitting, tumbling and crawling over each other in frenzied swarms.

Going back into the house, I found a magazine and rolled it into a tight baton. Starting at one end of the garden wall I began to pummel the flying ants.

It was dark by the time my father stepped out of the house and stood on the front street for a minute, steadying himself by the wall, and then pausing to light a cigarette.

My attack on the flying pismires stumbled to a halt, the rolled-up magazine flayed limp and scraps of torn paper embedded along the length of the wall amongst the pulped insect bodies. The evening had cooled, and as the darkness fell and the dew formed on the grass the living ants began to vanish. But long before their disappearance I had sickened of the slaughter.

On the near side of the garden wall my father stood, looking at the last of the broken specks of life obliged by the particular atmospherics of this night to fly.

"Why," I said. "Why do they do it?"

It was a minute or more before he answered. "They do it," he said, "to get in with company."

"Yes," I said. "But how come they ended up here?"

THE GIFT OF LUCK

On New Year's Day I was up early while my two brothers lay snug in bed. My younger and my older brother had red hair, but I had dark. And while people in our part of the world thought it unlucky to meet a red-head on the way to a cattle fair or at the start of the New Year, neighbours would offer bribes to entreat a dark-haired youngster to call.

With the smoke from the coal fires rising straight from the chimneys of the valley I set out. A first-footer. The token nugget of coal in my pocket and the gift of luck in my dark hair.

Snow had fallen overnight, with more snow on the way. For once, our dog wouldn't come with me, thinking it wiser to stay by the fire. As my boots creaked a solitary path through the snow I searched for the Devil's footprints. I'd been told that one year, after a heavy fall of snow, people found the hoof prints of the Devil in a trail that stretched across every field of every farm, showing where the Devil had walked the entire length of the country in one night.

There were no cloven hoof prints in the snow, only a line of paw prints, one straight in front of the other, the track of a fox. A magpie darted across my path. One for sorrow.

"Good morning, Mr. Magpie," I said to counteract its evil influence.

I had no fear. I walked with confidence and authority, vested with special powers in a snowbound world where magic held sway.

*

At midnight on New Year's Eve, with the snow just starting to come down, my father had aimed his shotgun into the bushes outside our front door and fired a shot. Around the valley other gunshots rang out to frighten off misfortune.

In Gaffney's field close to home there were stunted fairy-thorn trees that nobody would dare cut down for fear the fairies might come after them. The ring-fort in McNamara's land, I'd been told, had buried treasure hidden underneath a great flagstone protected by a demonic water-cow.

Even the reliable *Old Moore's Almanac* that listed Fairs and Marts, Tide Tables, and Early Closing Days for Irish cities, towns and villages admitted the supernatural. Along with the phases of the moon, various events over the coming twelve months were foretold: hurricanes and accidents with super tankers. And there were long-range weather guides:

If the cock moults before the hen,
we'll have winter thick and thin;
If the hen moults before the cock,
we'll have winter hard as rock.

The Almanac also advertised a method to prove you had a guardian angel. You could send away for lucky charms and pixies. Magic abounded. My horoscope for the month predicted a financially rewarding journey.

*

I called to Gilhooley's shop first. Mrs. Gilhooley gave me a warm welcome and a bag of liquorice allsorts sweets. In Guihen's house I got a shilling, tea and biscuits. Kate McKenna offered me sixpence and several chewy Emerald sweets. Mary Dyer – a woman who could cure a sty on the eye with a rub of her gold wedding ring – gave me a slice of Swiss-roll and another shilling. Tommy and Mrs. Tivnan gave me lemonade and biscuits, and a two-shilling bit.

Onwards then, to Baby Regan's house.

"Come in *a grá*," she invited into the kitchen.

I didn't know if my stomach could hold down any more kindness, but she was so happy to see me I couldn't say no. Every year Baby Regan, who was 70 years old or more, scattered primroses around her house on May Day and walked with her bucket to take the Flower of the Well first thing on May morning.

An hour later, I reached Martin Reynolds' house. His front door stood open and I found him inside chatting with his neighbour Johnny Guihen. Both men sat on kitchen chairs, holding their hands up close to the open fire. Martin had no electricity and in the dim kitchen their faces were rosy in the glow of the flames with a blue snowlight coming into the dark kitchen of the open door.

My arrival prompted the two men to start talking about the ghosts and apparitions they'd seen over the years.

No two living men had seen more ghosts in their day, or knew more about the world of the supernatural. Johnny said if you stepped over a crawling infant you would stunt its growth, which as I was small for my age, was probably what happened to me. Johnny also said a bee flying into a house meant a stranger was on the way. A robin in the house foretold a death. A dog's tail could draw lightening.

I stood with my mouth open as they recalled seeing Jack-o'-lantern lights over the bog while crossing the mountain. Johnny told me about a half-man/half-horse that only gave up chasing him when he crossed fresh running water at the bridge back the road. A bridge I would have to cross on my way home. Even Johnny's dog had the power of second-sight, and stood with its hair on end, barking at an empty spot in the road where a neighbour died suddenly. Another landmark I would have to pass on my way home. And Martin described how he went astray in Gaffney's field one evening. He said he stepped by mistake on a patch of famine grass, the *fear gorta*, and only found his way out of the field again when he turned his jacket inside out so as to confuse the spirits trying to lead him astray.

According to Johnny and Martin our town land had more ghosts and spirits than it had living people. Johnny said he visited a house one time where the baby never stopped crying. Day and night the baby kept crying until the mother and father were nearly out of their minds.

Johnny asked to see the child. He looked at the infant's face, contorted with howling. Then he went out into the yard and came back with a bundle of straw. Standing over the bawling child in the cot, he lit the straw and pushed the taper of burning straw into the child's face. A strange and horrible looking creature jumped out of the cot and ran out the door. When the mother and father went over to the cot they found their own baby asleep. The faeries had been trying to take their child and leave a *ceolán*, a crying fairy, in its place.

In the next breath he warned me: "Don't go trying that at home now, do you hear. And never look a ghost in the eye, son. Only the Pope can do that. If you meet a ghost, keep your eyes down, put out one foot and stand on its toe and ask: 'Where in the name of God are you wandering?'"

"I'll remember that," I said bravely.

The winter light was dimming in a gathering snow shower when I left the two old men sitting in a huddle close to the fire.

Alone on the winter's road, I looked over my shoulder and listened for the sound of hooves following me, until I crossed the stone bridge and the barrier of fresh water flowing underneath. And passing the spot where the dog had barked at the invisible presence of a dead neighbour, I felt a shiver of unnatural cold.

It began to snow again and there was not a house or another living soul in sight. Only the silence of the snow-covered fields and the rustle of fresh flakes falling and tapping on the hood of my anorak. The snow shower thickened and slanted through the bare trees; trees whose branches took on the shape of old men's heads. I felt an urge to run. My pace quickening, I suddenly took off in a race home to bright electric light, the company of my brothers and a comforting mug of hot Bovril. The first-footer money safe in my pockets but the magic spent.

THE MONEY CHANGERS

D-day arrived in February 1971 and the country went decimal. I loved taking the new money to Gilhooley's shop. A press of the button in the middle of the shop door made a bell ring at the far end of the private house. A minute or two later, Bernie Gilhooley opened the door into the poky, tin-roofed extension, attended only when a customer called. His shop at the foot of the mountain was small, but handy whenever Daddy ran out of Woodbine cigarettes, or if my mother needed Blue Band margarine or spaghetti hoops for the tea, or kippers in tomato sauce with a big iron key on the lid for opening the tin.

Prices varied.

"Hi, Tessie?" Bernie called for his wife as he retreated down the unlit passage between the house and the shop, waving my order of a half-pound packet of Halpin's willow tea. "Hi, Tessie, how much is this?"

"19 new pennies," she answered.

"19…19-and-a-half…" Bernie mumbled under his breath. "20 new pennies," the price rose steadily on the journey back.

Long before anyone ever heard about the new currency Bernie was known, when totting up accounts, to add in the day, the month and year at the top of the bill to the column of old money pounds, shillings and pence.

Along with the flexible prices, the shop was under-heated and damp.

"Mind would that spill," Bernie unwisely cautioned a neighbour one time when she was putting the pound of sugar in her shopping bag.

"Bernie," she said. "I could have kicked the last bag of sugar I bought here home in front of me, it was that hard."

The stove meant to keep the shop dry had a downdraft and Bernie was forever holding up sheets of newspaper to the front to improve the draft. When the sheets of newspaper caught fire, and the flaming newspaper had to be stamped out on the cement floor – adding even more smoke to the room Tessie warned him to go easy on account of his high blood pressure. Bernie maintained there was nothing wrong with his blood pressure; it was his new tablets that were no good.

Deep down, Bernie was enormously proud of his business. He once told my father that "a yard of shop counter was better than twenty acres of land."

If the smoky stove left Bernie choking for breath, and high blood pressure brought a rush of white spots before his eyes, this change over to the new currency really had his heart truly broken. How could a pound note that used to be worth 240 pennies be worth only 100 pennies in new money?

"The people have been robbed," he complained, forgetting the spontaneous price rises whenever he was in charge of the shop.

But I had come to play on Bernie's confusion, mixing old and new prices to my advantage.

"How many penny biscuits for a new penny?" I asked.

"One."

"A new penny is worth two-and-a-half old pennies."

"I don't care. I'm not giving you half a biscuit."

"What about the broken ones?"

I was not for hurrying in my choice of sweets, and I drove him out of his mind converting the price of Peggy's leg and sweet cigarettes, ice-cream wafers cut from the block, a bottle of Fun or TK lemonade, and Long John bubble gum with the free transfers the colour of bruised flesh that I used to tattoo my biceps.

"Are the penny chews a new penny or an old penny?" I asked, exercising my puny muscle over Bernie.

"What about penny drinks?"

"Get out, get out. I have a squeezing in me head listening to you."

"You'll have to get used to the new money, Bernie."

"It'll never catch on in Arigna," he vowed.

He began to praise then the old "ploughman" pound note, the "red lady" ten-shilling note, the "thrupenny bit", the tanner, the florin, the half-crown - generous coins with a noble Irish salmon and horse, a hen and her clutch of chickens on the face. He spoke of their beauty like a poet in his lonely rage against down-draughts, the doctor who changed his tablets and the "decimation" of ordinary people's money.

LEGGING IT

I was watching *The Six Million Dollar Man* on the television when a neighbour's child burst into our house. After he blurted his message, my mother sent me running out the fields to get my father.

I raced out the garden path, taking a shortcut through the orchard to reach the first meadow. As I ran through the fields to fetch my father, I was Steve Austin, astronaut; a man *barely alive*, but thanks to the men in white coats and a six-million-dollar budget, *better, faster, stronger than before*.

My father had been less fortunate than the bionic man, Steve Austin. Following an operation for "water on the knee", he had come home with a surgical scar the length of his right leg. A Government doctor examined the result and declared him unfit for any kind of manual labour. Unable to work as a full-time gardener or labourer, he was finally granted a disability benefit. But every so often he was spot-checked to make sure he was still unfit for work. And the neighbour's child had warned us there was an inspector in the district making a surprise swoop.

I pictured myself moving in the slow motion used by the TV series to capture the fleetness of Steve Austin's nuclear-powered legs. And having reached the first meadow field, I used my Steve Austin bionic eye to scan the neat rows of finished haycocks in the still strong sunlight.

There was no sign of my father and I had to keep running.

Earlier in the week my father had hired a man with a tractor and a fingerboard-mowing machine to cut the three best meadows on the farm. We had a lot of hay down, in an effort to save the entire crop in one sweep. The forecast was good. And I had been released for an hour only to watch *The Six Million Dollar Man*, while my mother made the evening tea for Granny and Grandad, and my father worked on alone in the hayfields.

In the neighbouring fields I could spot with my bionic-keen

eyesight other families saving hay in an all out effort to make the most of the fine weather.

Many of the men working in the fields were coal-miners. Some had genuine health problems, especially lung trouble; the result of rock dust, farmer's lung and cigarettes. But the hot weather reduced the demand for coal in summer months, and a lot of the pitmen with small farms went on disability benefit and "sick certificates" to get the hay saved.

I found my father in the lower corner of the last meadow. When I told him about the inspector he downed his hayfork, and though short of breath, he half-ran, half-hobbled towards the house on his bad leg.

I took off again. Imagining the rick-a-tick-tick special-effect noise of my super-powered bionic legs I cleared the neighbouring hedge in one breakneck jump. My sudden arrival and the message I carried sent coal-miners running from their hayfields like they were working underground - and I had brought news that the roof over their heads was about to fall in.

YANKEE PARCELS

We collected Green Shield Stamps. When we had the right amount of books full of stamps, we sent them off with an order and got back a household gift in the post. We never got anything bigger than a toaster but we liked to tease our postman, Jimmy Noone, saying we'd sent away for a wheelbarrow that he would have to push by hand from the post office up the side of the mountain to Crosshill.

Jimmy never had to contend with the wheelbarrow, but every so often an enormous brown cardboard parcel arrived that he had to balance somehow on his bicycle. We lived over halfway up the mountain and it was a hard push whenever a Yankee parcel came. Propped on the crossbar the cardboard sides of the parcel lost their stiffness with the moisture from his body.

Jimmy was forced to stop often to adjust his sack of letters and take off his cap to wipe the grime and scalp oil from the leather headband. But even in the hottest weather it was a matter of fierce pride that he wore his full uniform; the heavy navy blue trousers and brass-buttoned jacket, the hard peaked cap like a policeman.

His old-fashioned uniform conjured up associations with the early Irish Free State army and police force. And the uniform conferred a certain authority on our postman. He could report unlicensed dogs, unlicensed bulls, unlicensed televisions, or if you had a black and white television license even though you owned a new colour set. He could make a reliable guess at most of the business going on in a household by the number of official brown envelopes, domestic white envelopes or foreign stamped letters that came in the post.

Nan had a soft spot for Jimmy. All the women did. He was a bachelor who said, "Yes, Mam," and "No, Mam," when he spoke to the women. He carried news between their houses: deaths, accidents, whose children were off school or sick, whose cattle were on the road.

"Anyone who brings news into a house brings news out of a house," was Matt's guarded opinion.

Jimmy got tea from the women. Bread and jam if the household was busy, or Galtee processed cheese, a slice of tomato and a slice of fresh soda bread on better days. If he had letters for only one or two houses on the mountain he brought his own sandwiches: raw onion scattered thinly on white loaf-bread.

He was all smiles the day he brought an American parcel into our kitchen. It made him happy to be able to present such a hefty offering to my mother. And the parcel earned him a full dinner.

"You had some load on a hot day," my mother felt guilty because she'd put him to so much trouble.

"I'm kill't out with the heat, Mam."

"Rest yourself for a minute."

While she began to peel the potatoes Jimmy stretched his legs and took his ease, his boots shining under the table and his peaked cap left on the oilcloth.

They talked about the weather. Jimmy said he met Mrs. Gaffney the other day, running with a bottle of holy water in her fist to sprinkle on the roof of the henhouse as the storm was rising He watched her splash holy water on the loose sheets of iron being lifted by the gale. When she finished he said: "Would you like me to put a rope on that as well, Mam, just in case the holy water doesn't work?"

After the yarn, he glanced at his watch. He was on over-time now for the delivery of the parcel, and he fitted the metal bars of a Jew's Harp between his front teeth and began to twang out a tune.

We had to wait until Jimmy left before we could rip open the parcel. The softened cardboard tore easily, and the delay caused by the fortified bands of brown tape only added to the anticipation. On top there was a note for my mother, then the dresses, frocks and skirts. And Dime bars made from American chocolate with a mysterious, almost unpleasant flavour that harmonised with the smell of the clothes: a blend of exotic fabrics, camphor mothballs and ozone after the parcel's slow sea-passage.

Some of the clothes from America we could wear, like the T-shirts and jeans, but even the jeans were a funny shape. The dresses for my mother were so gaudy she would never dare to be seen out in them, and the men's jackets for my father were loud enough to frighten the cattle.

The garden path became a catwalk as we strutted in the American sequined gowns, the high heels, and the extravagant hats. We twirled and pouted in the costume jewellery for our own amusement. Wearing the long coats and boots, we did the goose-step and raised one hand in Nazi salute. We mimicked American Uncles in out-sized suits.

"God Damn!" "Somebody ought a do something." "You lousy bums."

It might appear that we were ungrateful, but the suits that perfectly fitted those barber-shop groomed men on the sunny sidewalks and broad avenues of America, the spangles, the taffeta, the gaudy fabrics of the women's dresses looked ridiculous in any other setting. Ireland wasn't ready yet for the brash individuality of these cast-offs.

And though we were always on hand when a parcel from America was opened, we never noticed what came for Matt and Nan under the lurid camouflage. Contraceptives. Forbidden by law in the Irish Free State, they came hidden in the American fashion magazines at the bottom of the parcel. And never once in all those years did our postman in his State-issue blue uniform suspect the kind of contraband he was employed to carry into our house as he smiled and waited for the spuds to boil.

OPPOSITES ATTRACT

When they took over from my grandparents the running of the farm on the mountain, my mother and father inherited Martin Reynolds. Martin had small dark eyes like raisins and a baby-smooth complexion, hairy nostrils and hair in his ears. He owned a single brown pinstripe suit, a Fair Isle slipover, a collarless Grandad shirt and a cap that only came off at meal times. He cleared his throat constantly. *Brrurrph… brrurrp…* he'd splutter as he walked the roads, tugging at the lapels of his jacket with his chest puffed out. A throwback to an earlier time of child-hiring fairs, itinerant labourers, tatie-hokers and spalpeens. Martin claimed the amazing feat of having once "walked the whole way home from Scotland back to Ireland."

When we knew him he was homeless. Or as he said himself, "When my cap is on, my roof is thatched."

He came to work around the farm years before when Henry Joe was building the new two-storey dwelling house with money got through a Land Commission grant. He employed Martin to mix cement, carry stones and lift the roof-beams. When Grandad asked Martin if he thought a joist had been cut the right length, if a wall looked strong enough to support the weight, if the pitch of the roof appeared too steep or too shallow, Martin gave the same non-committal answer: "She'll go or go down, Sir."

Granny was obsessed with collecting eggs. Every chance Martin got, he downed tools to inform Granny he had just heard a hen cackle after laying out. She immediately dispatched Martin to find the nest. Off he went with a hand-hook to poke the ditches. The minute he was out of sight he lay down for a snooze in the long grass.

Once, when Granny took over the job of finding a laying hen herself, she brought Martin along with her. They could hear the hen cackle in the undergrowth but they couldn't see her. Granny swung the hand-hook to clear away the briars and accidentally swept the head off the hen. As the severed head went flying past her shoulder, Martin said, "You're getting warmer."

Granny often lost her temper with Martin, and she never let up about his drinking. The opening hours on Sunday increased, and the pub owner, Mick Flynn, built a new extension to accommodate the bigger crowd after second Mass.

"Flynn's pub has made a great Catholic out of you," Granny said to Martin. "Every pound you leave on that man's counter puts another slate on his roof."

"When you have health and wealth," Martin said, "you don't need money."

Granny had a very poor appetite. To ease her bad stomach she took spoonfuls of Glauber's and Epsom salts, Milk of Magnesia, Bisodol, Andrews Liver Salts and went through whole packets of baking soda.

Martin had a stomach as strong as a cast-iron firebox. He ate his stirabout laced with salt, he ate salted herrings, salted country butter and salted bacon and there was never a word about heartburn, hardening of the arteries or high blood pressure.

When the dinner was ready, Martin took off his cap and moved his chair in close to the lower end of the kitchen table. His favourite dinner was boiled cabbage with wads of fat bacon and flowery spuds bursting out of their jackets. He had a steady but neat way of eating: peeling his spuds with delicate relish, adding great nuggets of salted country butter and washing the whole lot down with mug after mug of buttermilk.

Granny spooned a small portion out on her own plate and picked at it while sitting with a hump in her chair by the fire. When she left her plate aside, and went to the dresser to make up another concoction for her stomach, Martin eyed her and said: "When the firebox goes, you're bucked."

Granny fed Martin less out of charity than out of a sense of her own importance. She imagined herself a big farmer, with 23 acres of land on the side of a mountain and labourers from the council cottages who worked on her land for their dinner and a drop of milk to bring home in the evenings. She also hired a hackney man to take her to mass on Sundays.

The regulation fast, from midnight on Saturday until receiving communion on Sunday at first mass, was as nourishing to her as the feed of bacon and cabbage was to Martin. She drew strength from starvation and the sight of her neighbours fainting in chapel and having to be carried outside to be revived.

While Granny was full of religion she was short on ordinary kindness. It was Nan and Matt who gave Martin a place to live: an empty house that belonged to a bachelor called Charley Duignan. Charley died before the house was finished and Granny had urged Grandad to buy the property for the land and the turf-rights on the mountain that went with it. The house had a good slate roof, sash windows and a front door. The walls inside were painted with two bands of distemper: pink next the floor and yellow next the wooden ceiling with a strip of ornamented border paper in between.

Conditions were basic, grim even, but Martin found it better than the old people's retirement home.

Once, he had to be hospitalised for a week for a chest infection. After his discharge, the ambulance dropped him off at Nan and Matt's house. He arrived with his thumb split open after he got it caught accidentally in the ambulance door. Martin thought this only a token of the treatment he'd receive in an old people's home.

Martin had no electricity and no running water where he lived, but he hadn't far to carry his gallon of water from the spring well beside the house. He had no neighbours and his toilet was the fresh-air variety. He lived according to the amount of daylight, getting up when the sky turned bright outside his window without curtains and going to bed when the sky got dark.

"What does any man need only a bed and a pair of shoes," he said. "If you're not in one you're in the other."

He fuelled his open fire with turf stolen from the mountain.

"Martin," granny lectured him one day on the consequences of his thieving. "Do you know where men who steal turf go?"

He looked at her with a straight face and said: "If a man couldn't find it around someone's house, he'd have to go to the mountain."

An alternative to the stolen turf was Martin's cock-shot. He would perch an empty beer bottle on the garden wall next the road. The colliery lorry passed in the evenings, taking the miners home from work with the last load of coal. As they drove past the pitmen lined up with lumps of coal to break or knock over the bottle on the wall. Knowing Martin, they used big lumps of coal to pelt the cockshot. After the lorry passed Martin went out with a bucket and gathered up the spent ammunition, enough for a warm coal fire for the night.

Martin had no religion, but he was very superstitious. Living alone on the mountain, he claimed he heard the voices of the dead at night, along with fairy music and ghostly set-dancing around the roofless barn at the gable of his cabin. Martin begged Matt and Nan not to remove a single stone from the same barn after the night he struck a match to light his pipe and saw in the flare of the match a big white cow standing in the middle of the abandoned barn and a tiny little woman doing the milking. Another evening, on his way home from the pub, Martin said he got hit by a 'fairy blast' of wind that tumbled him head-over-heels into the ditch.

Every form of apparition had a name; the good people, the little people, the *forgeen marrows* and the *bo dans*. A rank and file of supernatural creatures as elaborate as Granny's orders of angels, martyred saints and apostles.

Granny and Martin were opposites in every way. Granny had her savings in the bank, her communion on Sundays, her holy days of abstinence and denial, her bad stomach, and a heart as joyless as a headstone.

Martin, on the other hand, arrived at a wake-house one night to console a man whose wife had been a tyrant while she was alive and had never shown Martin the slightest kindness.

"She's gone," the distraught husband lamented as he handed Martin the expected glass of whiskey. "Ahh! Martin, she's gone."

Martin raised his glass and said: "Devil the harm, Sir."

The difference between Granny and Martin was so profound it amounted to a romance. And Granny did get a good one back at Martin after he spent the day in the pub and arrived in her kitchen, empty handed as usual.

"Would you not think of buying something for the morning," she gave out to him.

"A man could be dead by morning," Martin said.

"Would you not buy a loaf of bread," she said, "just in case you were alive."

Granny died first, and suddenly, from a heart attack.

Martin, when he got older, was re-housed by the Government in a blue wooden prefab. He lived the rest of his notably long life in comfort.

Until the end he walked to the pub for his bottle of stout every day in a new dark suit, a topcoat and a broad-brimmed hat that made him look as if the village had appointed him Mayor.

Granny's sudden death meant that she missed having her final confession heard. Against this omission she had countless foreign mission masses said for her over the years, donations made to the church, fasts observed and indulgences gained. But when our grieving Grandad asked Martin what he thought Granny's chances were of getting into Heaven after the pious life she'd led, Martin tugged at his lapels, cleared his throat and said, "She'll go or go down, Sir."

PLOUGHING SEASON

Grandad was outraged when he saw the heavy loads of manure being hauled by donkey and cart to the meadow for the plot of ground my father had set aside for the potato crop.

"Look at the sweat on that poor donkey," he said.

My father wiped his forehead with the back of his hand and said, "What about the sweat on this poor donkey?"

Our existence relied on ploughing. Every spring the breath of newly turned clay filled our house the way the tang of the sea invades the homes of fishermen.

The blade of the plough became polished from use. At dusk the plough, the coulter and mortarboard were loaded back on the cart and the tired horses led into the barn to cool. The steam rose from their flanks in the half-dark as I carried buckets of water to the rhythm of their steady chomping from the nosebags full of oats and barley. Working through Easter and the fast days of Lent, the horses were sometimes better fed than the labourer. An arrangement that provoked one hired ploughman to say, 'If I'm offered another boiled egg, Missus, I'll never be able to look a hen in the eye again.'

At the start of March we took shelter behind a windbreak of hawthorns from the raw east wind, as we split last year's potatoes in half to make our buckets of seed go further. We planted potatoes by the acre, with bent and aching backs, my father steadily scooping shovel-loads of clay to have the crop in before Saint Patrick's Day and the embarrassment of a late or "cuckoo" crop. When the tender rosettes of the early leaves appeared on the ridges we could only pray they wouldn't be scorched by an unseasonable frost. We then had the job of "moulding" the potatoes with a second covering of clay to promote a faster growth, followed by the heart-lightening relief of seeing the crop mature without the hungry spaces of failed seed.

Early summer, and my mother said she could think of no garden plant lovelier than the flowering potato stalks. In the afternoon I liked to crawl into the middle of the potato crop, roofed in by the lushness of the stalks. There I lay on my back with folded arms looking up at the moving clouds, vividly aware of the process of growth and flourish, decay and renewal, in this green and unhurried corner of the mind of God.

"June is the month when the dog fell off the ditch with the hunger waiting for the new spuds," my father said as we rooted for small, early tubers to be cooked and eaten in their flimsy jackets, their intense nutty flavour enriched with a knob of salted butter. As the spuds got bigger, we made *calais*, a mound of mashed potatoes with chopped scallions fresh from the garden and a hole in the middle for a pool of hot milk and melted butter.

In July we hauled the 40-gallon barrel of water and the heavy but wondrously gleaming bags of crystals out to the field to make the bluestone and washing soda mixture to ward off the blight. A barrel-full of mixture as blue as the sky above, with summer insects and chaff from the meadows floating on top. My father strapped the copper sprayer to his back and walked in his oilskin trousers through the musky, army-truck green of the leaves and the dripping and abundant stalks. The sun and a warm breeze dried the mixture into a milky glaze. Wood pigeons cooed in the sycamores humming with bees.

Hard and hand-blistering work occupied us all summer in the hayfields. And then, through August and September, the hay had to be brought in to the shed, the haycocks "snigged" in from the meadows with a loop of rope tied to the ass collar and hames. As each bench of hay rose higher, my father forked from the ground and passed the forkful of hay to my older brother who stood halfway up a wooden ladder. He gave the fork load to me, doing the tramping and the building in the heat and dust under the iron roof. The hay harvest finished in time to start digging the potatoes.

By late autumn the potato stalks were wilted and brittle with decay. The granary hedgerows shone rich with berries: snowberry, blackberries, haws and rose hips.

We dug the potatoes by turning back each side of the ploughed ridge, "hoking" the tubers from the clay, and leaving them to dry in the middle of the ridge with their backsides to the wind. Our hands were perished by the wet clay. Above our heads a pair of ravens gave tongue to the bell of blue October sky. And my breath caught at the impact of that autumn light, radiant beyond the ordinary.

In our part of the country, by custom and necessity, the potatoes were left out in the fields all winter, stacked in heaps under clay sods with a thatch of rushes. But we had a spare outhouse that we used as a larder for the autumn work. Opposite the potatoes were the cooking apples in cardboard boxes, hand-picked from the trees in the orchard and resting snug on pillows of straw. The base of an old-fashioned wire spring bed hung in the rafters to make an airy loft for the onions and shallots. The spade, the wooden hay rakes and pitchforks with iron prongs polished by the summer work rested at an angle against the wall, the familiar weight of their seasoned handles left up for the winter.

With the summer and the autumn work done, and a ripe Halloween-apple and dry-hay smell in the misty yard, Grandad in his last years used to walk as far as the hayshed, climb the wooden ladder and sit on a high bench, smoking his pipe and looking out at the gloom and drizzle, a picture of contentment.

Winter fell hard. North winds blistered the skins of the haws. Magpies darted through snow-filled skies like bad omens. The hills were as hungry as grey crows in a famine. We had months of carrying ropes filled with hay on our backs to the cattle wintering out in the fields. We brought the cattle in at night only when it snowed, bringing fodder by the arm-load into the barns in the evenings and again in the mornings. The warmth of the cows lingering inside the barns after they were turned out for the short day. The diamond crust of the snow lying in the yard sprinkled with straw and hayseed richly fragrant with summer.

There were all kinds of hungry mouths to feed. Not just the farm animals, but small birds with lemon breasts, blackbirds, song-thrushes, robins who followed and befriended us for the winter season, all waiting for boiled potato skins and raw potato peelings. The cock pheasants reared and released into the wild by my father for the local gun-club scraped the frozen potato ground and flashed their magnificent scarlet, emerald and golden plumage. When the dog caught their scent they gave a shrill cry and took off, the brisk air whistling in their feathers.

We survived too on a diet of potatoes; boiled and mixed with cabbage to make colcannon; a country egg mashed through the potato to make bruisey; left-over mashed potato and flour and salt for Potato Cakes, or pratie bread; potato salad made from chopped up cold potatoes and a dollop of Chef salad cream for the Sunday night supper, together with a slice of pork luncheon meat. Grated raw potato to make boxty.

Boxty on the griddle, boxty on the pan
If you don't eat up your boxty
You're not a Leitrim man.

Was it a healthy diet? The thought never occurred to us. We ate everything that was put in front of us.

Deep winter and all life moved indoors. Grandad sat close to the fire in the low light with a ball of cobbler's thread, mending ass collars, bridles and breeching. He also sharpened blades and corrected the teeth of a saw with a file. A buckled scythe blade had to be hammered into shape. The hatchet and the hedge-knife blades were rubbed surgical sharp with the emery stone, and a hay-rope twister was put away like a precious family heirloom.

The amount of time Grandad lavished on essential belongings made his generation of old men with homemade lids on their pipes remarkable. They left nothing out to rust. Every tool had to be oiled and maintained; the way soldiers confined to barracks looked after their rifles. A lifetime of work-worn character in every hand-tool that gave such a deep feeling of timelessness to this farm world, right as a furrow and old as the clay.

THE PERPETUAL MOTION MAN

He spent his life on a farm but at heart Grandad was an inventor. As the jobs piled up on the land he plotted ball-bearing races, tracking the movements of flywheels and pendulums to crack the problem of perpetual motion - a machine, or the motion of a machine, that would work indefinitely without receiving new energy.

Grandad inherited a good dry farm of land on the mountain. And Granny must have thought she did all right when she married him. She never guessed that in his top pocket Henry Joe McDermot carried a slide rule for making scale drawings and a wooden ruler that measured inches in big black numerals and unfolded on brass hinges to convert abstract ideas into experimental prototypes. Nor guessed that he was only happy when he had his rulers and his pencils and a notebook open, pouring over the schematics of another hopeful system of pivots and fulcrums.

When granny lost her patience waiting for him to tackle more mundane household jobs, she mocked him with dear Liza's comeback in the song about the hole in the bucket: "Well, fix it, dear Henry!"

Henry Joe had four daughters and one son, Bernie Joe. But Bernie Joe never saw eye to eye with Grandad. One time when Grandad made a suggestion on how to repair a Lister diesel engine, Bernie Joe told him, "If you said that to our ass, he'd kick you."

"At least," said Grandad, "he'd have the manners to listen."

Bernie Joe joined his sisters in America.

*

Grandad took an enormous amount of time shaking out wisps of hay in the meadow field until they fell in even layers. Then lifting them on the prongs of his fork, he turned them in mid-flight, forkful-by-forkful, as the haycock went up with the precision of a master mason erecting a steeple. Then the haycock had to be trimmed around the butt and headed off with a cap of wet green hay and the sides raked to the waterproof finish of new thatch. With the haycock built he sat at the butt, his lap full of straw and fed wisps to the hand-twister while we walked backwards and away from him as the hay rope spanned the air between us. The placing and the tying of the hay ropes went on for the rest of the evening.

The art of hay rope-making was really in the hands of the person feeding out the straw, like wool going on a spindle. But Grandad had perfected a lightweight, low-cost twister made from strong-gauge "bull-wire" bent into the shape of a starting handle with two tubular grips improvised from black hose-pipe. We loved using the twister, and we also borrowed tools from Grandad's workshop wholesale to make up for the shortfall in our own toys.

Invading his workshop, we manufactured from whitethorn branches the flintlock pistols favoured by the highwayman Dick Turpin and the space age "phasers" out of *Star Trek*. We made Winchester and Springfield rifles from used floorboards, and car steering wheels, Apollo rockets and moon landing craft from Grandad's reserve of bull-wire. We even made a stab at a replica of the flying sub from *Voyage to the Bottom of the Sea*. In the process, we blunted the blades of his chisels, bent his tri-square, lost his rasp and wood saw and broke the handle of his claw-hammer. We could never get our hands on enough nails. There was no tool belonging to Grandad we didn't finally damage, mislay or lose out the fields. Not even his wooden ruler was safe from a trick we had where you had to unfold the ruler away from your body in three moves.

As Grandad got older the trip to collect his and Granny's pensions became his one big remaining chore. The job took all day.

First, Grandad had to round up the ass, Jackie, and get the bridle on Jackie's head, a manoeuvre that often required several laps of the pasture field. Then the tackle had to go on the ass: the hames, straddle, breeching and chains. Then the loading of the cart began with a bundle of hay and a bucket with water for the donkey, an emergency back-up rope and a flour-bag stuffed with straw for his seat, plus the shopping bags, and perhaps a cog-wheel or axel that needed to be dropped off along the way for welding into a revised perpetual motion machine.

As lengthy and painstaking as the preparations for the trip might seem, they were nothing compared to the writing of the shopping list.

Seated once more at the kitchen table, Grandad first had to light his pipe, cleaning and scraping the bowl scrupulously with the small blade of his penknife, scouring the shank with a pipe cleaner, cutting tobacco next with the bigger blade of the penknife and feeding the flakes with this thumb from a hollow in the palm of his hand. Then striking a match, he sucked and popped his lips on the stem, drawing and puffing smoke with the satisfaction of a man taking his ease after a day of unmerciful labour.

As the wag-the-wall clock swung from tick to tock and back again to tick, the stub of pencil he kept in his velvet-lined eyeglasses case had to be pointed, his glasses polished, his penknife sharpened on an emery stone, then a smoother oilstone. He then had to make tiny squares out of a sheet of paper taken from an airmail writing pad. Finally, he declared himself ready to have the shopping list dictated to him by Granny, who sat waiting all the while in her chair beside the fire, her thumbs spinning like twin propellers at a speed greater than anything Grandad had yet to contrive in his workshop.

When Grandad arrived at the shop, he handed in his list over the counter and went to the bar next door. There he met the sons of the men he had worked with before he retired from the coal-mines. As the pitmen "washed down the dust" after work, they stood Grandad several drinks, paying for every round of drink with pound notes black with coal dust from being carried about in their working clothes all day. In return Grandad entertained them with riddles.

"A father dies and leaves his three sons seventeen horses." Henry Joe would launch into that week's riddle with the pitmen gathered around him. "The will states that the oldest son has to get half the horses, the second son gets one third of the horses and the third son gets a ninth. But the half of seventeen is eight and a half and you can't have half a horse."

"You could have a half-share in horse," a pitman pointed out.

"But what about the other sons; they have to get a third and a ninth."

"Could they not sell the horses and divide out the money?" another pitman asked deliberately to get a rise out of Henry Joe.

"Man dear!" said Henry Joe, throwing his hat on the floor. "Who mentioned anything about selling horses?"

The dafter the answers to his riddle got, the more indignant he grew at the ignorance marshalled against him, never asking himself what mark of intelligence it was to be quizzing pitmen out for a few pints in the pub after the day's work.

As his shopping was loaded on the ass and cart outside, Henry Joe enlightened his audience by introducing a jockey to the riddle. The jockey added his mount to the seventeen, bringing the total to eighteen. The first son lead away nine horses: the half of eighteen. The second son took away six horses: a third of eighteen. And the third son got two horses, his ninth share. "Nine plus six plus two equals seventeen, and the jockey walks away with his own horse," explained Henry Joe.

After which he settled his cap back on his head, untethered the donkey and said, "Giddyup".

The next day Henry Joe suffered. Though he never drank much, Grandad got terrible hangovers. The wooden settle-bed in the kitchen had been replaced by a mysterious *chaise longue* that we called the long-settee. And here was his resting place the day after his evening in the pub. With a pounding head and full of pity for his tender condition, he stretched out full length on the long-settee and moaned the whole day with his face buried in the leatherette.

"What's wrong with you?" asked a neighbour one evening after she rambled in for a chat.

"It's his bad back," Granny said.

"There was nothing wrong with his back yesterday evening," the neighbour blurted, "when he was waltzing around the pub."

"*Clob mór*," was all Grandad could groan as Granny launched into an attack until he had to rise and leave. Driven from the house, he stood in the front garden looking up at the clouds: the mare's tails, goat's hair or mackerel-patterned cloud that concealed from him all his life the mystery of tomorrow's weather.

The years passed. Granny died. And Grandad persevered without success in his workshop. But at the age of 74 he set one last plan in motion. He took a flight to see his son, Bernie Joe, in Chicago.

In his son's timber-frame home in the suburbs, he examined how the central heating and the air conditioners worked. He posed for a 16mm home movie with his son, daughter-in-law and grandchildren. He shook hands with Mayor Daly. In the cool of the evening he sat in the back yard and marvelled at the size of the mosquitoes. As the darkness fell he spotted the glow of fireflies amongst the mosquitoes under the trees and said,

"We're in trouble now, they're coming looking for us with lanterns."

Towards the end of the visit, Grandad stood with his son on a bridge above a freeway. Together they watched the torrent of car headlights streaming through the night in apparent endless motion. Later, over a glass of whiskey, Bernie Joe made it clear he would not return to the farm on the mountain.

Grandad came home with a toolbox full of hardware to replace the tools we'd lost and broken. Maybe he had fresh ideas to realise after seeing the perpetual traffic on the freeways of America. But his kidneys began to fail.

Settling into his room, he applied himself to the job of dying with the meticulous approach he practised in his workshop. He lined up his medications on the bedside locker beside his pens and pocket watch, his slide rule and a packet of Oatfield sweets. He thanked my mother for looking after him. He made it clear that she, and not his son, would inherit the house and the farm of land.

"When all fruit fails, try haws," she thought to herself. But she gave a solemn oath to her father that she would look after the home place. And so through his daughter, Grandad succeeded in a way that he never plotted or anticipated in his notebooks - for within every model of continual motion is the need to perpetuate, to preserve and pass on.

THE SHOP

We were never without a copy of *Old Moore's Almanac.* Between its green paper cover the Almanac listed sheep fairs and cattle fairs, fair days and half-days in shopping towns throughout the country. Why we bothered with the Almanac I don't know, we knew precisely where and when to sell our livestock, and the local shop was an absolute fixture in our world

This was a general shop of the kind where the iron bar inside the door was lifted and the sunlight was first across the threshold. If there was nobody waiting outside the shop the floorboards got sprinkled with water to keep down the dust. But most mornings my father or some other man stood waiting on the doorstep to buy cigarettes or tobacco: ten Woodbines or a half-quarter of Bendigo Plug. Bought on tick.

There were two kinds of tick: put it on the clock, or mark it in the book. The notes kept on the top of the clock were taken from pads made up the night before from the plain newsprint used as packing between the layers of cigarette boxes. The clean paper was carefully straightened, folded and cut with a knife to make short-term credit notes, kept together with a wooden clothes peg.

Longer-term credit got recorded in the ledger with the sheet of blue carbon paper worn flimsy from making counterfoils. The orders were simple: loose-leaf tea, meal, sugar, pipe tobacco, custard, clarinda or 'injun meal' and flour. A lot of flour. There were few customers for the token batch loaf or two. Everybody baked. The newspaper came by standing order only and had your name written on it. Clients returned their newspapers when they had them read and the pages got used for wrapping. Brown paper was rarely used, except to make up parcels or a Christmas box.

"Sir," we said to the shopkeeper.

"What part of the country are you from?" a shopkeeper asked a young lad who had the nerve to call him by his first name. "And have they no manners there?"

Along with the groceries the shop sold lumber, bicycle parts, Wellington boots, gallowses, socks, wallpaper and paraffin. The timber had to be cut to order on the spot, and the customers were often women like my mother who got fed-up waiting for the man at home to do the job. Her knowledge of carpentry might not be exact but she could picture the finished job. Hands measured air while she explained: "I need a bit of timber about so big."

"Six by four?"

"Lighter than that."

"Two by one?"

"I'd want stronger than that?"

"Two by two?"

"That'll do."

"Would you need twelve foot?"

"I wouldn't want all that."

"Four foot?"

"Another bit."

"Eight foot."

"Can you cut that in two?"

This process went on until the shelves or the cupboard took shape. And even more time was needed to convince her how much timber sold by length made up the pile at her feet.

Bicycles needed to be maintained and so the shop sold bicycle chains, tubes, tyres, freewheels, mudguards, ball bearings, valves and valve rubber, flash-lamp batteries, reflectors, dynamos, spokes and spare wheels and bicycle outfits. The bicycle outfit looked beautiful. A shallow tin box with curved ends holding a selection of patches, emery paper and a mini-grater for the little block of French chalk, a tube of solution and ball-bearings. A bicycle-driven social order encapsulated in one box.

The Wellington boots hanging from the ceiling had to be retrieved by their string ties using a long pole with a brass hook on the end. And their brand new rubber smell soured the first time the insides got wet.

A host of smells filled the shop: the waft of blue and pink paraffin from the yard; bluestone and soda crystals; the dry tannin smell from open tea-chests; boiled sweets; boxes of loose biscuits, including ginger nut, thick and thin arrowroot. You had vanilla essence for cooking alongside cans of red lead paint for carts and iron roofed sheds, and balls of creosote-steeped ropes for haymaking. Not to mention the pungent jute and hemp cart ropes measured in arms lengths or fathoms and sold by weight.

Everything was sold by weight. Saturday nights were spent weighing out the sugar in bags, plain paper bags tied at the top with string, every shopkeeper being versed in the art of looping and smartly snapping off the required length between their fingers. Brass and cast-iron weights with lead inserts balanced the fan-faced weighing scales and their exactness was liable to official inspection. When trade was in old money, six tomatoes on the enamelled scales weighing fourteen and three-quarter ounces at one and three halfpence a pound meant you had to be quick at totting up in front of customers who watched like a hawk and could read upside down.

The sides of bacon were preserved in layers of salt that turned liquid in the summer heat. Nobody would buy the bacon unless it had a good honest layer of fat, and the shopkeeper could upset customers trying to fob them off with too much lean bacon. With salted bacon and salted herrings came a need for the white enamel buckets that made water carried from the spring-well glimmer crystal clear to the bottom. Porringers were popular, as were the tin cans made by the tinkers. The tin cans that the boiled sweets came in were useless. The bottoms leaked and dropped out of them in the heat.

Connemara woollen socks were sold loose, and the needles for darning came in an attractive card like a bouquet of flowers; the needles inside arranged by size in a sheet of shiny red-foil paper. The device for threading needles also cleared the jets of a blocked primus stove perfectly. For the needles you needed thread: spools of number 8 and number 10 black and white hand-sewing thread. Hand-washing got done using packets of Rinso, together with a corrugated scrubbing board, a hard brush and a bar of Sunlight Soap for scrubbing the collars and cuffs.

The pharmacy area had Beechams and Mrs. Cullen's Powders, Max Smile razor blades and Lifebuoy pink carbolic soap. The Lux, Palmolive and Nivea beauty soaps were displayed in a separate cabinet and were counted luxury cosmetics. Very few toilet rolls were sold. A travelling rep who left the shopkeeper stuck with a load of toilet paper came back trying to flog toothpaste. "If they won't buy paper to wipe their backsides," the shopkeeper said, "They're hardly going to buy toothpaste."

People used baking soda to clean their teeth.

A greater demand existed for the rolls of tar-paper used as an underlay to keep back the damp and smooth out uneven walls beneath the wallpaper. The shop stocked a variety of wallpapers for the hall, kitchen and drawing room. Hall paper had vertical stripes, kitchen paper had fruit or harvest scenes, bedroom wallpaper had sloping patterns, and drawing room paper had to be heavy-flock or embossed.

Men like my grandfather, Henry Joe, always gave their shopping list in over the counter. And the first thing to be handed out was the tobacco. Occasionally, a rush of customers arrived at the same time: five or more men handing in lists on their way to the bog or the hayfield. The shop closed for dinner at one o'clock. And no matter how late the doors closed, the shop opened again at two. The front door closed at eight in the evening, after that you gave a rap at the side door if you were stuck for something. Wednesday was a half-day.

Farm wives bartered with fresh eggs, rhubarb and cooking apples. Nobody bought milk. But the notion of convenience food and instant meals began to take hold amongst the younger generation, even if everything came dried or in cans.

We persecuted our mother to treat us to packets of Birds Dream Topping, Instant Whip, Vesta dried beef or chicken curries, and Fray Bentos Steak and Kidney pies in cans heated in the oven – 'snake and pygmy' pies we called them. Soon, we were cooking for ourselves packets of dried Roma spaghetti boiled in water for fifteen minutes, then doused in tomato ketchup with a few pan-fried sausages thrown in, and to crown this feast, a whipped up concoction of Angel Delight.

More outlets began to open, and more people owned cars to take them further a field. The large general shop lost its importance. The notion of choice became established. People continued to run up tick in the local shop, but they might not be seen again for months. They didn't have to come back. And the more money they owed, the more likely they were to stay away.

The shutters finally closed, the iron bar went across the front door and the clock with the pile of unpaid credit notes on top wound down. The shop stood still while the people moved on.

TOM SWIFT AND THE AMAZING AI MAN

I had my head stuck in a book of science fiction called *Tom Swift and His Amazing 3-D Telejector* when my father told me to call the AI. The decision to try artificial insemination, instead of walking our cow to the nearest bull, was my father's idea to improve the quality of an ageing herd. Holding the exact amount of coins for the call hard in my fist, I raced swiftly to the nearest telephone.

On reaching the shop at the foot of the mountain I blurted to the owner, "Hello Mrs. Gillhooley, we have a cow on the rambles."

She escorted me to the public phone and wound the handle on the side to rouse the post office switchboard. The switchboard called the main exchange. From there the operator called the AI's local dispatch office. Knowing if I got it wrong I hadn't the price of another call, I gingerly fed my coins into three different slots and pressed button A on the moneybox. The right order of coins went down. I was through to the AI.

"When did you notice her?" they asked.

"This morning," I said.

"Is it her first time?"

It never occurred to me to ask was our cow a virgin. I wasn't even sure I was supposed to know what the word meant.

"I think so," I stammered. Realizing only after I said it, that what they wanted to know was whether the AI had been called out before to inseminate the same cow. There was no charge for a repeat call, but it was a black mark against the AI to have too many repeat calls resulting in late-spring calving.

"Watch the Skies!" American B-movies warned citizens against alien spacecraft arriving to conquer our world. I kept an equally keen lookout until a car pulled up in our farmyard and I shouted: "The AI man is landed."

Ignoring the warning to "keep out from under the man's feet", I watched him extract a slim tube from a canister wafting its dry-ice haze like the liquid oxygen and nitrogen teaming from a Saturn V rocket on the launch pad at Cape Canaveral.

With a clear plastic glove reaching up his arm, the AI man took the tube to our cow in the barn. Afterwards we left out a bar of carbolic soap, a hard towel and a bucket of lukewarm water for him to scrub up. Apart from this simple courtesy, a docket and the discarded launch tube were the only trace of his visit.

We watched the cow closely but she showed no signs of a second heat. Nine months later we were watching the cow again. There was not a corner of the farm I did not know by heart and when I noticed our cow searching for hiding places, my mother told me she was picking out a place to have her calf. A short time later the cow's udder packed out and the "pins dropped" as the hipbones changed position for the passage of the calf.

I led my mother to the hiding place. We got the cow up on her feet and my mother coaxed her in from the fields. A "waterbag" had already appeared and our cow stood stock still in the barn, big-eyed and chewing the cud, sick with the pangs of birth.

Whispered debates between Nan and Matt took place in the yard on the proper moment to intervene. Any unnecessary commotion could unsettle the cow and postpone or even threaten the delivery. Wait too long and the outcome might be equally devastating.

Throughout those fraught hours, my father hunkered in the yard and smoked several cigarettes. Finally he said the cow was in difficulty. My mother asked if she should run for a neighbour to help. My father said there was not time and he swooped with a rope and looped it around the only part of the calf to have appeared yet, the front hooves.

What followed was a heart-stopping tug of war before the calf choked on the fluid in its lungs. I joined my father pulling on the rope, oblivious to the cow piss and the dung and other fluids. It astonished me how hard we could pull and still the calf wouldn't budge. My father used his bare arm to locate the head. We pulled harder. And then miraculous the calf slithered smoothly free and hit the straw in a glisten of afterbirth. Its mouth and nostrils were cleared quickly by hand and the hanging tongue stirred in protest at being dragged roaring into the world. A beautiful, fawn coloured bull-calf.

Furthermore we had a totally new breed of animal on the farm: our first Charolais-cross calf. The future had arrived - not in the form of 3-D telejectors or the flying saucer I longed to find secretly landed in our far meadow - but in the shape of an AI man up to his elbows in animal health and worried about repeat calls.

A PHOTOGRAPHER SHOWS UP

The coalfields of North Roscommon were, for Adam Woolfitt, another element in a straightforward assignment for the *National Geographic* to document life along the length of the Shannon River: the waterway and its people, economy and geography. But when he got to Arigna he had two problems. First, the coal miners didn't work on Mondays. Secondly, Arigna wasn't the industrialised mining town he expected, with smokestacks and redbrick terraced housing.

Instead he found a tranquil river valley with family-owned coal mines scattered amongst the sandstone foothills. The surrounding farms were tiny and cheerful as strings of bunting improvised from upland meadows, rough pasture and swathes of bog teeming with wildlife and native shrubbery. Most of the coalminers, it turned out, were small farmers also. When he asked why so many followed both trades they told him: "The miner always kept the land, but the land never kept the miner."

He decided to photograph the landscape and come back another day when the coal mining resumed. But a mist came down the mountain and the river valley vanished under a blanket of fog. On the verge of putting away his camera equipment he heard a mysterious noise. A donkey and cart appeared out of the gloom, the iron rims of the cartwheels making a grinding sound as they incised twin white lines on the damp road.

A man with a loose hold on the bridle walked at an easy-going pace alongside the donkey and cart. A small dog stood out on the end of one shaft of the cart, swaying in balance with the motion of the donkey's slow progress. Despite the poor light, Adam Woolfitt couldn't pass up this ideal picture. He wiped the condensation from the lens and raised his camera.

My father often brought strays back to the house. He never learned how to drive a car and he relied on the young lads who worked in the coal-mines to give him a lift home from the pub. In springtime, men would arrive at the house to buy the bundles of Early York or Flat Dutch cabbage plants he sold off the farm for extra income. On mart days, cattle dealers brought him home and in return got a pot of tea and a ham sandwich to clear their heads after a day of hard bargains. Once one old-timer arrived on a World War Two dispatch rider's BSA motorbike. He was looking for fresh parsley for a kidney problem, and had been told that Matt Leyden was one of the few men in the valley with fresh parsley growing in the garden.

Another evening, my father landed home with Sally, a mongrel terrier pup asleep in the pocket of his tweed sports jacket to replace Harvey who had passed on after a gruff and stiff old age. Sally lived for over sixteen years and accompanied all three children into manhood. Then there were the lambs rejected by their mothers who we had to bottle feed by hand: cute bundles of wool with black snouts who took over the household like new babies. Another night, my brother Terry came home after seeing *The Exorcist* and met face to face in the dark with the beard and horns of a buck goat my father had won in a card game and chained to the road gate until he could break the good news to my mother.

When Matt led Adam Woolfitt into the kitchen, my mother had sheets of newspaper spread out on the kitchen floor to walk on while the freshly mopped linoleum tiles dried.

The photographer said he worked for the *National Geographic* and he was hoping to take a few pictures. My mother stared mortified at the newspaper on the floor.

By an odd coincidence, she was familiar with the *National Geographic Magazine*. Her sister Teresa sent my mother a 12-month subscription from America as a present one Christmas. The *Geographic* journals were meant to help with the children's education, but the articles were so meticulously fair-minded we never read them. We preferred to look at the photographs and thought taking pictures of penguins and polar bears for the *Geographic* in the Artic Circle one of the coolest jobs in the world.

My mother hated having a camera "stuck in her face", but she didn't want "to do the poor man out of a living" either. Especially when he worked for the *National Geographic*, a publication so important you needed the signature of an existing member to take out a subscription.

"You'll have me disgraced," she said.

"Just be yourself," Adam Woolfitt coaxed and aimed his Nikon.

Before leaving at midday he asked if he could call back when the weather improved. He would pay for his board and keep and stay with them for a day or two if that wasn't asking too much. It was. Nan told him politely but firmly she didn't have the room to spare.

When we got home from school she told us about the photographer. We were so disappointed we'd missed him we gloomily decided we'd never seen him again. But my mother felt relieved not to have this inquisitive stranger hovering over her shoulder and prying into the family's private affairs.

Adam Woolfitt returned the following Saturday. He brought a packet of twenty Woodbines for Matt and a box of chocolates for Nan. Flattered by his thoughtfulness, they felt obliged to give him a tour of the farm.

He used up a roll of film on the cattle barns alone. And his attentions delighted my mother, whose arms still ached after giving the walls an emergency coat of whitewash with a tablet of Rickett's blue for added brilliance just in case the photographer showed up again.

In the barn he arranged the cow chains in loops by the timber stakes polished smooth from the cattle scratching their necks in the stalls. Intrigued by the atmosphere of quiet order and connection with the past in the dusky interior of the stone-built barn, he included in the background the cast-off donkey shoes, horseshoes and nameless bits of iron stuck in the masonry gaps. A barn where each animal had a pet name that my mother rhymed off: Kane's cow, the White Cow, the Blue Polly, McPoleon and the bossy Queen of the herd. In this barn, too, each animal had a regular stall they took up of their own accord when led in from the fields for milking in the morning and again in the evening.

Adam Woolfitt took close-ups of Nan and Matt's firm grip as they hand-milked each cow, finishing off the "thinnings" down to the last pale "skite" into the froth of the overflowing buckets of milk; milk with the distinct herbal flavour of sorrel and meadowsweet, from the rich autumn after-grass. For this strong milk the creamery gave a quality bonus. The secret, Nan explained, was to cool the milk as quickly as possible.

The moment they had the milking done, the buckets were plunged into cold water and left to cool in a stone water-trough fed from the depths of the spring well that supplied the house. The bonus was very important to Nan, and she was enormously proud of her creamery cheque. This pride was her quality control.

Scalding the insides of the creamery cans with a boiling kettle, my mother said that from early summer until the after-grass finished in late autumn they could fill almost two ten-gallon creamery cans. For the rest of the year they would be lucky to fill a single creamery can. The household income rose and fell accordingly.

No tampering influenced this cycle of winter shortage and summer plenty. Few medicines were used. Except perhaps for a tube of penicillin to prevent mastitis when the cows went dry or a tablet for white scour for the young calves. The warble-fly dressing programme had eradicated that pest, while outbreaks of black leg and red water were a thing of the past and foot and mouth still a remote horror. The terms were unknown, but in almost every respect they produced free range and organic food, its quality and flavour unrivalled.

The tour moved to the pig-shed.

"The 'murties' is our pet name for the pigs," Nan said.

"Whenever I look at the pigs," Matt said, "I think of Jim Ward, who said to the pig in his yard, 'I don't know whether I should kill you and eat you, or sell you and drink you'."

The pigs used up the skimmed milk that came back from the creamery every evening, but Nan said she resented the damage they caused. They rooted holes in the pasture fields and poked their snouts under the flagstones and dislodged the tidy paving done by her father.

Matt said nothing.

The tour continued past the hen house where the Rhode Island Reds and Black Minorca hens roosted safe from the fox at night and scratched about the yard all day. They looked into the old dairy where Nan's mother had churned the homemade butter before they started to send milk to the creamery.

Adam Woolfitt got a surprise when he spotted the grey Ferguson TVO tractor parked near the hay barn.

"The ass is easier started in the mornings," Matt said.

"Matt leaves the driving to the boys," Nan explained.

"You have to look to the future," Matt said. "Not like her mother who told me the evening I landed home with the tractor, 'You've bought yourself a heap of trouble.'"

"She was old and set in her ways," Nan said.

"And when the row broke out, who got the blame?"

"She could be cranky," Nan said to Adam Woolfitt. "Sometimes, when the children were small, they got under her feet."

"If we hadn't moved in with them in the first place, the trouble would never have started," Matt said.

"It couldn't be helped," Nan let it go at that, afraid she'd disclosed too much in front of a stranger.

They hoisted between them the ten-gallon creamery can full of milk, Nan with her free hand grabbing her hip to counter balance the physical weight. The milk in the can went to the local creamery at Kiltoghert. First, it had to be delivered by ass and cart to the crossroads at the foot of the mountain. There the creamery cans with the individual supplier's numbers painted on the lids and sides stood like stout army reserves in tin hats for collection by a man called Charley Gaffney.

Few people in the area owned tractors, and Matt could hear Charley coming before he saw the plume of black exhaust from the labouring engine. He gave the reins of the ass and cart a shake to synchronise their arrival.

Charley talked to himself aloud, pushing his dentures out on the point of his tongue as he made slow headway on his tractor with the flatbed-trailer loaded with a cargo of creamery cans. Delays happened when he got into an especially loud argument with himself and his dentures popped out all the way and had to be retrieved from his lap. Yet Charley and his chesty diesel engine tractor and rattling trailer were the lynchpin of this economy as compact and functional as a three-legged milking stool.

In the afternoon Matt went to the field to dig potatoes. The stalks were wilted. A mother-of-pearl haze hung over the countryside. The Kerr's pinks he dug straight out of the ground with a spade flashed brightly against a red plastic bucket. Matt wore a brown jacket and trousers, his working suit. A handsome, fair-haired man in an open-neck shirt, his boots glazed from the damp pasture and the tops of his socks out over the cuffs of his trousers. The camera clicked. A hundred years after the Great Famine and the potato remained the mainstay of his smallholding.

The red plastic bucket appeared again in Matt's hand in the evening. He stood aside while Nan proudly led out the new Charolais-cross suck-calf with her first and ring fingers stuck in the calf's mouth. She had her headscarf tied under her chin and a blue nylon housecoat on. She was laughing heartily and Matt's answering smile went deep under his cheeks. A couple in their 40's, confiding their business and airing their grievances to that most neutral of onlookers, a professional photographer. A couple long past the first romantic notions of love with rows and tensions like any other family where three generations had gathered under the one roof. But pulling together to keep that roof over their heads and to see their three children had warm meals and clean clothes, stability and a good education, so that they might escape this same drudgery. A couple bound by money worries, animal welfare, the weather and hard work. Unselfconscious and proud of their stock. A couple married to the land. And as my mother told Adam Woolfitt wrapping up the last shot, "It's too late now to go looking for another partner."

THE DESTRUCTIVE ELEMENT

THE WEARING OF THE GREEN

I was a Provo before my voice broke. At school concerts and on stage in the local hall, or whenever the Americans were home on holiday, I rattled off songs about the armoured cars and tanks and guns that came to take away our sons. I serenaded the memory of James Connolly, that true son of Ireland, his life for his country he bravely lay down. I lamented the fate of the man sentenced to Dartmoor for 21 years. I went off to Dublin in the green in the green, where the helmets flashed and the rifles crashed to the echo of the Thompson gun.

In the schoolyard I told jokes current in the North about Jesus being born in a manger because the proddies had all the houses. I could recite:

Up the long ladder and down the short rope,
To hell with King Billy and God Bless the Pope.

And in my spare hours I searched the mountain for secret caches of Civil War weapons, "Peter the painter" automatic pistols, Lee Enfield rifles, spare ammunition and hand-grenades. I found vantage points: elevations from which to conduct an ambush or lob a mortar at an invading army convoy.

My fascination with guns, rebel insurgency and IRA active-service units continued into secondary school were I met Master Griffin, a spare and upright man who wore a fedora and eye-patch. He had a distracted air, seeming only to address himself whenever he told his stories about the struggle for Ireland and for freedom. But he had a great knowledge of local history, especially the War of Independence and the Civil War, retelling incidents such as the Keadue ambush, when the North Roscommon Brigade, including a man called Paddy Gannon from Arigna, "winged" Sergeant Riley and captured three rifles, a revolver and ammunition from an RIC bicycle patrol on their way to investigate a staged robbery in the village of Ballyfarnon.

And yet, if Master Griffin came across acts of vandalism in the school he would shake his head and blink his one good eye, muttering under his breath in Irish: "*Ah sea*! The destructive element – Ah yes, the destructive element."

One morning during the break I encouraged a friend to skip our history teacher "Dry-Balls" class to go to the funeral of an old-time Republican. Rumours were going around that the old soldier would be buried with full military honours.

We sneaked downtown and made our way to the church choir-loft that we called "the gallery". Looking down, I was amazed to see at the head of the congregation several men dressed in black polo neck sweaters, black berets, dark glasses and handkerchiefs tied around the lower part of their faces. They were standing to attention on either side of the coffin draped with a Tricolour.

Two priests celebrated the funeral mass. The second priest, whose family came from the North, traipsed in one door beside the altar and out the other door several times during the service, banging the doors as he went.

We followed the cortège to the cemetery where the IRA men fired a volley of pistol shots over the grave. A couple of plain-clothes detectives wearing bright plaid shirts and sheepskin coats watched from an unmarked car. The Special Branch detectives known as the "Heavy Gang" for their methods of interrogation and the size of their beer bellies were meant to be incognito but even I could spot them a mile off. They maintained their surveillance of the crowd but held back even when the pistol shots were fired. I enjoyed seeing the Heavy Gang powerless before the defiant mourners.

After the funeral we sneaked back to the school. The main building and the surrounding prefabs were silent. Everybody was back in class again after the break. We tried sneaking around the side of the building and ran straight into Master Griffin.

"Where were ye?" he brought us up short.

"At the funeral, Sir."

"*Ah sea*! Get along to your class, now."

My mother and father did not encourage strong political feelings of any shade or persuasion. But television brought us pictures from the North of civil rights marchers suffering indiscriminate baton charges and needless violence at the hands of the RUC and B-specials. We felt the Irish army should be sent in. At the very least the nationalist people had to be given arms to defend themselves against the rampages ignited by Ian Paisley. And despite reservations over the state of her hair I became a great admirer of Bernadette Devlin.

Repeated showings on TV of Edward Daly waving his white handkerchief for mercy from gung-ho British paratroopers as he lead people to safety during the Bloody Sunday massacre made my fists tighten with rage. And there was a quality of gleeful mayhem about the protest burning of the British Embassy in Dublin following Bloody Sunday that made the struggle against perfidious Albion a lot more exciting than the sorry embers of failed insurrections and traitors to the cause raked over in "Dry Balls" official school syllabus history class.

Many of the men who worked in the Arigna coal-mines had staunch Republican credentials. At the height of the Troubles, a rumour went around that explosives from the various coal mines were making their way North. The "Heavy Gang" division of the Special Branch kept an exceptionally tight eye on dissident elements in the valley; neighbours were followed by unmarked cars that prowled the valley at all hours of the day and night. It was a subversive act to be caught reading, never mind selling, a copy of the Sínn Fein paper, *An Phoblacht*. A coal-miner was 'lifted' for selling glue-on official IRA or "Sticky" Easter lily badges, whereas my crowd, the Provos, used a pin to hold their green-white-and-gold paper lily badges on the lapel.

In the North, internment without trial of Republican sympathisers and the raid-and-ransack tactics of the British Army seemed violations of justice that could only be answered with equal force. Later, the protests by the 'men on the blanket' and the death of Bobby Sands and nine other hunger strikers gave the Republican cause a purity of intention that answered the malignancy of Margaret Thatcher and her Government of Tory running dogs. The black flags all over the country, the towns shut down, the broken glass and crowd-control barriers in disarray on Dublin's O'Connell Street were eerie yet powerful indicators that our day had arrived. If somebody would only hand me an Armalite rifle I was ready for active service.

It seemed inevitable when a stolen truck after an armed raid found its way to Arigna. The raiders tried to hide the truck in a disused coal mine but the roof of the mine was too low. If they had asked for my expert local knowledge, I would have told them to let the air out of the tyres for the truck to squeeze in.

Knowing that the truck had been found but no money recovered, I searched the nearby hiding places, hoping that my sleuthing skills would unearth the missing loot and maybe an automatic pistol into the bargain. When I told my father and mother what I was up to, they said "Curiosity killed the cat". I laughed at their misgivings. Then a man who reported finding the truck to the authorities came upon a fallen tree blocking the road as he was driving home one night. Getting out of his car to investigate, he was nabbed by hooded men who covered him in black paint and feathers.

A few days later, my father brought me with him to go pigeon shooting.

There was what we called an "alt", a ravine covered in scrub wood, not far from the home place. In the evenings the pigeons flew in to roost in the larger sycamore trees. After we entered the alt, he directed me to cut light hazelwood branches while he plucked ferns and sprigs of ivy to camouflage a hide. Before climbing into it to wait for the pigeons he handed me the shotgun.

The gun had a dead weight quality, the heavy gunmetal barrel and carved wooden stock balanced in the middle by the gracefully curved trigger and firing mechanism. Step by step he showed me how to handle, load, shoulder, and aim the shotgun. And how to be responsible for it.

"You carry a shotgun with the barrels pointing towards the ground," he said. "And you slip off the safety catch only when you're ready to fire. Never bring a loaded gun into a house. And never ever point a gun at another person."

He made me repeat this etiquette until I knew it by rote. Then he directed me to stand close to a sturdy hawthorn bush and shoulder the gun. I levelled and aimed along the barrel, tightening the gun into my shoulder as

I got ready to fire. After the imaginary gun battles of my childhood I was finally positioned to use the real thing.

The weight of the shotgun put an incredible strain on my extended arm. The barrel wavered and I was forced to apply fierce concentration to keep the target in my sights. An easy squeeze of the trigger produced a tremendous kick that would have broken my shoulder if I hadn't the gun correctly braced. The bang was deafening and there was a surprising amount of blue smoke. And when I looked at the tree, the lead shot had ripped through the bark, mutilating the white timber pith and toppling over the tree, its trunk broken in two.

"That's the kind of harm a shotgun can do," my father said. "Imagine that's your leg or someone's head or chest. Imagine the harm you could do."

From that evening onwards I could ask for the gun whenever I wanted to go hunting. I stopped looking for IRA arms dumps and developed a proprietary interest in maintaining my father's shotgun. I squirted liberal amounts of 3-in-One penetrating oil to keep the mechanism smooth while using a rag on a string as a pull-through to clear corrosive smuts from the barrels every time I fired a shot. I rubbed the stock with lavender floor polish and loved the spent cordite reek so much I would sniff the jagged end of recently fired Eley cartridges.

To hone my hunting skills I got out books from the mobile library on the art of rough shooting and fancied myself a crack shot. I became an early riser, out without a breakfast, a shotgun on my arm and a red cartridge studded belt about my waist. An armed lord of the fields I went tracking a fox that nabbed one of our hens. But the old fox bettered my young running enthusiasm. All I ended up with after a long chase was the beak, scattered feathers, and coxcomb where the fox had already stopped for breakfast.

Throughout this period the bombings, sectarian executions and reprisals on all sides persisted in the North: 17 dead and 182 people injured in the Birmingham bomb. Bombs in Guildford and London. Bombs in Dublin and Monaghan that left 34 people dead and over 200 people injured. A bloodletting on all sides so dreadful and so merciless it threatened to split the bedrock of any shared humanity.

"They went mad in the North again last night," people at home said when they heard the latest news from BBC Northern Ireland and

Ulster Television, where every newscast ended with a warning for shop holders to return to their premises to check for incendiary devices – if they still had a premises to return to.

But despite our proximity to the North, the atrocities reached us second-hand. The distance between the actual border and the home place acted as a buffer as the violence escalated on the other side of the RUC roadblocks and the British Army surveillance towers. The pain and grief and terror suffered by the people of the Six Counties were mediated through television, radio and newspaper accounts. Even so, we began to feel lucky to be out of it.

Then one hot summer day towards the end of August 1979 I was working in the hayfield with my father and brothers. We kept seeing small planes and helicopters flying over the field headed in the direction of Sligo. Eventually news came through that the IRA had blown up Lord Mountbatten's boat off the coast of Mullaghmore. His 15-year-old grandson, a 15-year-old friend and a 17-year-old boatman had also died, along with the Dowager Lady Bradbourne. And there had also been a deadly ambush at Warrenpoint where 18 British soldiers were killed by a landmine.

It took that scale and proximity to make the violence real.

Yet when the British army set about blowing up "unapproved roads" to seal off border crossings between the North and South, a busload of volunteers from Arigna travelled North to fill in the craters, more for the entertainment value and a day out than from any burning political conviction. We blitzed the roads with white paint and "Brits Out" slogans, but Republicanism around home had the quality of a cat-and-mouse game with the law that dodged and blurred the underlying murderous violence.

There was a raid then by armed robbers on the two shops and the pub in the village. Locals were forced to lie on the floor while the robbery was in progress. But instead of outrage at this violence, a story surfaced about one of the older women clients in the shop. Her nerves were bad and as the robbers waved their guns, yelling at people to stay down on the floor, she whispered to the coal-miner sprawled on the floor beside her: "Are they going to shoot us?" To which he said, "You can be certain sure of it, Mam."

When the racehorse, Shergar, and the businessman, Don Tidey, were kidnapped in the same year, the search for both eventually moved to our part of the country. Roadblocks ringed us in, and house-to-house searches were started in the run up to Christmas. But the searches were more ridiculed than resented. And everyone knew about the response of a harmless bachelor, Tommy the twin. When an armed policeman stuck his head under Tommy's single bed, Tommy asked: "Are you looking for the stallion?"

Another man was brought to court after the guards found *poitín*-making equipment during the house-to-house searches. His solicitor said the *poitín* still had been covered with dust and obviously hadn't been used for a very long time.

The Justice accepted this point, but said the defendant would have to be fined for possession of the equipment.

The man stood up in the middle of the court and said: "You might as well sentence me for rape while you're at it. I have the equipment for that too."

The Justice doubled his fine on the spot.

Republicanism represented a deeply ingrained mistrust of all forms of authority: the higher powers of police, welfare inspectors, means testers, veterinary inspectors, banks, big business, politicians and Government departments, anyone trying to poke their nose into a person's private dealings. An attitude encapsulated by the tight-lipped burlesque outside the town chapel when a television reporter questioned a line of Ballinamore men in County Leitrim following a shoot-out during the rescue of Don Tidey from a bunker in the nearby wood that resulted in the death of a soldier and a garda.

Pressed by the reporter and camera crew for an opinion, every man gave the same answer:

"No comment... No comment... No comment..."

Being a "no comment" Republican was not the same as being in collusion with terrorists. It was like being in on a secret. Being one step ahead of the authorities and knowing something important they didn't know. Republicanism expressed a fundamental lack of trust in all forms of authority. It was a weapon against anyone tempted to exercise too much power over our lives. When we said we were against British rule in Ireland, it meant we weren't too keen on having our own crowd telling us what to do either.

BALLROOM BLITZ

Sex turned out to be an even more powerful and subversive weapon than anything the IRA might hold in their bunkers. For some time now I had been living a double life, like a terrorist who gave the appearance of being a normal person while secretly keeping back terrible knowledge of magazine rounds stashed under the mattress. In my case, *Playboy* magazine. As my voice deepened I left the "Men Behind the Wire" to sing with more feeling about the girl with eyes that shone like diamonds. My imagination roving from the rattle of Thompson guns to the upper-crust allure of Lesley Anne Down in *Upstairs Downstairs*.

Hot pants had come into fashion in what seemed an endless succession of hot summers, along with Kangas and skimpy tops tied with a knot above the navel.

On one such summer evening I stood at a crossroads. At the junction of the Dowra and the Convent Road in the town of Drumshanbo, Declan Moran had a shop where he repaired and sold motorbikes. My brother Terry wanted to buy a second-hand Honda 50 - what we called a "chicken chaser". And even though I knew absolutely nothing about engines, I was there to help him pick out a bargain.

When we finally settled on a bike Terry asked if he could take it for a test drive. Declan Moran gave him the loan of a helmet. Terry clunked the Honda 50 into first gear but swiftly tiptoed up through neutral and into the higher gears, speeding off like Evel Knievel up the hill and past the Convent of the Poor Clares. I stood outside the tin-roofed shop, looking up the road and waiting for him to return safely. Sooner than expected I heard a Honda approaching on the lower Dowra road. I wondered how Terry could have got around faster even than the racer Barry Sheen.

The driver turned out to be an older man with a pillion passenger on the back of another Honda 50. They pulled up short of the spot where I was standing and the passenger dismounted. When the passenger's helmet came off her hair fell loosely around her face. A face so gorgeous she could have been a sister of Lesley Anne Down.

I couldn't take my eyes off her as I watched her hand her father the crash helmet and her coat. He bundled both away in the back-box. Then he turned the bike around and headed home while she walked from the outskirts into town. I knew instinctively it was an arrangement to spare her dignity - that she was on her way to meet friends and she didn't want to be seen arriving on the back of her father's "chicken chaser".

She nodded as she walked past. I caught her eye and she caught mine. And I never noticed Terry arrive back until I heard Declan Moran tell him the splutter in the engine was related to the timing.

Every bonfire night, on the 23rd of June, the coal-miners burned heaps of car tyres at a crossroads at the foot of the valley. There was accordion music and tunes from the local members of a drum and fife band. All kinds of people stopped at the crossroads over the course of the night. Around midnight I spotted the girl from town in the light of the bonfire.

I was tongue-tied after I walked up to her but she amazed me by asking straight off, "Are you the fella who goes around with a shotgun frightening the life out of innocent rabbits?"

"Wascally wabbits," I said.

She laughed and I opened my bottle of 'Fun' lemonade and offered her a swig. She said her name was Mary. It turned out I hadn't spotted her before because she was away most of the time at Boarding School. But any hopes I had of dating her were dashed when she said she was going away to spend the summer with her cousins in Donegal. We swapped addresses but nothing came of it.

In September my nose was back to the grindstone in the school metalwork room before a letter arrived. In the letter Mary said that life for the boarders was hard. The nuns only allowed her to rinse her socks and wash her hair once a week in cold water. Every Sunday she was forced into a room where she had to sit and write a proper letter home that the Head Nun censored before posting. It was worse than internment, she said. But the girls wrote letters to their boyfriends under the blankets with a flashlight after lights out.

S.W.A.L.K. wrote Mary at the end of her letter: Sealed With A

Loving Kiss. The prospect of a loving kiss made me fantasise about being not on the blanket but under it, with Mary, in a dormitory full of girls scribbling lusty love notes. But she confessed in her letter her fantasy was to escape downtown to buy a bag of chips.

I.T.A.L.Y. she wrote in the margin – I Trust And Love You. But I suspected that to save face amongst the other girls, she had to have someone to write to and the cryptic initials were only part of the formula. I agonized over the decision but finally decided not to write back. I had my pride too, after the long summer without a word from her.

It was Mary who broke the stand-off with a letter before the Christmas holidays. She wondered if I'd be in the Mayflower Ballroom in Drumshanbo on Saint Stephen's night.

My army bargain jumper with the canvas patches on the elbows and the shoulders had to go. An Indian stall-holder supplied me with the necessary cheesecloth shirt to go with my bell-bottom jeans and my beloved black vinyl bomber jacket. After a visit to the unisex hairdresser, a slap of Brut aftershave on the cheeks still raw from shaving with my father's safety razor, and a swipe of Mum deodorant under the armpits, I was ready for my first visit to the Mayflower Ballroom.

I'd been to dances and monster bazaars in the parish hall but I'd never been to the Mayflower - it was too big, too far away, too intimidating. But now I had a girl to meet. That left me with two problems. First, it was a teeming wet night, I had no transport and the Mayflower Ballroom was ten miles away. Second, you had to be over 18. Girls had no problem getting in: they enticed the men from the pubs. But young lads who showed up drunk or rowdy were considered a nuisance.

I pleaded with my older brother, Terry, to give me a lift to the Mayflower on the back of his Honda 50. He agreed. But when he saw the cut of me, dressed from head to toe in oilskins to keep my vinyl bomber jacket dry, he said that when we got to the Mayflower I had to pretend not to know him.

We stopped on the outskirts of the town and I left the oilskins in a bundle strapped to the carrier of the Honda 50. The helmet I brought with me. While Terry got two tickets I waited at his shoulder. He passed a ticket to me and I went ahead with the full-face helmet on, giving the ticket to the collector inside the door. I could dimly see the crowd inside through the misted visor, until a tap on the shoulder stopped me in my tracks.

"Do you want to check the helmet into the cloakroom?"

"*Nuuhhhh hanks*," the fogged-up visor muffled my reply.

I kept going with my head down.

Once inside Terry joked that it might be safer to keep the helmet on, as it was said that in the Mayflower Ballroom the men took a break between fights for a dance. A bunch of young lads were already jostling each other beside the toilet door, while the sullen-eyed girls ranked along the sidewall pretended not to notice.

Trying to look invisible I searched the cloakroom, the mineral bar, the dance floor and the balcony. There was no sign of Mary.

Crossing the dance floor I narrowly missed the mineral bottle dropped from the balcony that hit the man beside me on the head.

The row started straightaway.

The injured man and his friends and the gang from the balcony divided into factions, lining up on either side of the dance floor. Somebody shouted to me, "Mark your man and come out fighting."

The breeze from the punch that came in my direction was enough almost to knock me off my feet, but I ducked in time and thankfully it failed to connect.

"Hit him again in the same place," a voice called.

"The rebel hand was raised and the heather blazed," shouted a coal-miner as the bouncers pounced to break up the row.

The dancing stopped. The band took a break and went to the supper room.

I stepped speedily around a bouncer in a black tuxedo who had my neighbour in a headlock. "I have me man," the bouncer yelled to his associates as the ringleader of one faction went down in a cloud of thumps and Hi-Karate aftershave before being skull-dragged off the floor and tossed out the emergency fire-exit doors by the "hasp of his arse".

The band came back on stage and the music resumed.

Mary was looking across at me from the other side of the dance floor. When I went over to her she said, "You looked funny in the middle of all that fighting."

"Come here for a laugh and you'll go home in stitches," I said, amazed I could still make her laugh. But I was anxious too, knowing that for our date to succeed I would have to ask her out to dance.

We chatted for a while, watching the older and more practiced couples out jiving. The man bending at the waist, his backside pushed out and the beer-belly dropped low below the belt, while a jiving partner spun like a top around a casually outstretched hand. The woman in an ecstasy of twirls, the man offering only a token shuffle and swivel of the wrist.

When Joe Dolan launched into "*O me, O my, you're such a good looking woman,*" I asked her out on the floor. Some said that Big Tom was better if you wanted to jive. Or Philomena Begley. Not forgetting Margo, Brian Coll, the Cotton Mill Boys and Roly Daniels. But Mary worshipped Joe Dolan as he sweated up a holy rolling fever in a skin-tight shirt and Pentecost-purple suit.

After the show Mary had to collect a signed photograph and a signature in her autograph book to show to the other girls back in boarding school. I stood looking on scornfully as the old *roués* from the band in shiny suits and braided velvet jackets moved in on the women.

The night was getting on and now everybody was looking for a man with a car and a lift home. It seemed Mary had memorised the make, registration and owner of every car in the district and she pestered several fellas for a lift. Anything to avoid the humiliation of having to walk the wet roads home after the dance with spatters from the road up the back of her white jeans.

Outside, we were so hot after the dance there was steam rising off our bodies through our clothes. But I was shivering all over. Gangs of girls were in competition now for the remaining seats home, the girls being better than the lads at signalling what they wanted without getting into a fight.

My brother Terry came up to me. "What are you doing?" he asked.

He had a girl along with him and I handed her the helmet. "I won't be needing this," I said. "I'm seeing someone home."

In fact I had done a head count and reckoned there was no place for me in the car that was about to leave with Mary. The Ford Cortina was already far down on the springs and there wasn't an inch of room to spare in the back. I couldn't imagine a greater calamity, or a greater enemy at that moment than the car owner, this motorised usurper of my girlfriend.

"Get in you clown," the driver yelled.

The other passengers squeezed up on the seat and Mary made room for me by sitting on my lap. I banged the door shut. The ballroom lights went out. We moved off in the dark.

We were barely past the speed limit signs when the couple next to us got intimate. I panicked, knowing that I didn't belong to that league of specialists who could open a girl's bra with one hand, a manoeuvre the fella beside with the love bites on his neck executed with a touch as deft as Christiaan Barnard going about a heart transplant.

Mary pressed deeper into my lap. In my ear I caught the close heat of her breath. My hand touched bare skin under her red-wool jumper and moved upwards between her shoulder blades. Despite the excitement of this advance, I knew if I didn't get a slap in the face - and she really wanted me to go further - I'd fumble until she lost patience. I felt doomed even as we embraced. But applying the same delicate pressure used to slip a shotgun's safety catch; I felt the clasp opening up. Our lips met and I yielded to her disarmingly tender kiss.

OPEN LINES TO NORA

Every telephone call in or out of the village went through the post office switchboard where Nora was the woman in charge. Nora's post office counter was also the village well of gossip where everyone got pumped for news.

Customers were graded and served according to the quality of their information. Anyone who could report a sudden death was given top priority, but there was always the danger of being out-manoeuvred by a neighbour with the right times for the removal and the funeral. If you were in a hurry you could lure her interest with news of a stroke, a scalding, or an inconclusive medical examination. A gallstone or gall bladder problem might entitle you to a stamp.

There was a waiting list of up to five years to have a private telephone installed. Only a select number of homes had the telephone, and even then each house relied on a coded ring on an otherwise open line. Then the telephone numbers went double digit and the post office switchboard began to resemble an up-turned plate of spaghetti. A green and yellow painted cement kiosk appeared in the village of Arigna.

The telephone in the kiosk was as black and solid as a cast-iron frying pan and much the same weight. A kind of starter handle sprouted from the side that you had to crank up to buzz the post office. Then you lifted the big handset from the cradle to hear Nora drawl:

"Aaaarrrrignaahhh."

If you were lucky.

In a bad mood Nora might leave you cranking the handle on and off for at least ten minutes while she finished her cup of tea and ginger-nut biscuit. No amount of twisting on that spindle would be answered if a hot story started to break on another line. You had to have the patience to quit and ring again in ten minutes. If you tried to lift Nora out of it, by cranking up the handle and letting her know you were in a temper, you might never get through that day.

Once you got through to Nora, you told her where you were ringing from and where the call was going, surrendering names, numbers and townlands where family, business and love interests lay. Then you replaced the handset in the cradle while Nora buzzed her friends Angela or Dolores working in the main exchange. And there you stood while Nora, with a fresh cup of tea in her fist, caught up with the news from further a field. You could make small talk, study the scenery or finish the crossword in the paper, but you couldn't hurry Nora.

The safest course of action was to have your money ready, and I used to ease the tension of the long wait by stacking my change next to the three different slots in the top of the coin box. Finally, Nora tugged the long nosed jack-plugs from their housing, stretched the cords in a criss-cross pattern around the switchboard and made the connection.

The harsh clatter of the telephone in the kiosk made me jump after the long silence, and I lifted the handset once more.

"Insert your money," Nora ordered.

My girlfriend Mary was waiting on the other end of the line, but there was no way I could speak until Nora collected her dues.

The coins dropped through hinged trapdoors and inner workings and the high plinking note of a bell declared the procedure complete.

"Insert another five pee."

"It's gone down."

"Try it again."

"I've already put it in the slot."

"I didn't hear it."

"It's definitely gone down," I said mortified.

"Connnnecteeeed," Nora finally drawled.

She had let me off the hook, but not before I knew I owed her a juicy tit-bit the next time I stopped at her post office counter.

To even the score, we set a trap for Nora.

"How is the weather there?" I asked Mary.

"It's glorious here today. The sun is splitting the stones," she gave the prepared answer.

"That's strange," I said. "It's spilling rain here. Isn't it Nora?"

"It's coming down in buckets," Nora said without thinking. An instant later we heard a click loud enough to damage an eardrum as she pulled the plug on her headset.

The line was clear for the time being, but we would be idiots to trust our deepest love secrets, our most intimate affairs or our most confidential business to those humming telephone wires criss-crossing Nora's school-desk-sized switchboard. And I would have to pay the price for catching her out the next time I cranked up the phone to buzz the exchange, and then waited out my sentence in the kiosk.

THE FABULOUS MCHUGH HIMSELF

In a decade of free love I was constantly overcharged. Stuck at home, I didn't know what to do with myself. Mary, my girlfriend, had left me for a fella with a car. I felt moody, idle, and bored all the time. A thunderhead of pressure rumbled inside my skull. Trapped and sluggish, I felt unable to fit in or escape.

Every film broadcast after nine o'clock at night on the television had a nude scene, especially if it starred Alan Bates or Helen Mirren. The entire drama output of BBC 2 seemed obliged to have at least one naked tumble, despite the protests of that stout guardian of morality on the TV, Mary Whitehouse. Did these frequent and explicit sex scenes I watched throughout the 1970s condition my notion of beauty and sexual preference? Probably not. The first fully naked woman I ever saw was Glenda Jackson.

On the home channel, Gay Byrne and *The Late Late Show* sent Irish Bishops and self-appointed censors into tantrums of indignation for airing filth during studio debates with vigorous audience participation and phone-ins where mostly cranks and die-hards bothered to call – the liberals were probably too busy out having sex. For as one old man said when asked by a television reporter what he thought about sex in Ireland: "I think it's here to stay."

In between the empty-headed hours in front of the television, I walked the roads or took a book out the fields to read when the weather turned warm. Outdoors, the red-bodied insects in the meadows copulated non-stop amongst the suggestive gobs of "cuckoo spit" left by the grasshoppers on every stem and stalk. The family dog, in heat, coupled with passing strays, the donkeys on the road mounted each other willy-nilly, and every character in every book I read went about having casual, reckless and life-fulfilling sex.

There were few teenagers my own age around, and I suffered both mental and physical isolation. The nearest cinema was 15 miles away. We had no café or coffee shop in the village. It was a long walk to the shop even to buy an ice cream. The biggest gathering of young people outside school all week happened after mass on Sunday.

Saturdays went by watching the wrestling on the English stations: Les Kellet, the Royal Brothers, the masked mystery wrestler, Kendo Nagasaki, Giant Haystacks and Big Daddy. But the only excitement came when the dirty tactics of the tag teams brought grannies with tinted hair and handbags rushing up to the ring to intervene after a crowd-pleaser got mauled. Another weekend to kill and not even a decent or indecent film on the television. But I kept watching. Anything. Anything to easy the loneliness.

I hungered for space and freedom. When I grew out of my clothes they could be replaced, but no world I could find fitted the face now spotted with acne, with a haircut like a cheap nylon wig, looking stupidly back at me from the mirror.

But comfort arrived unexpectedly in the form of a sleek, lightweight transistor radio. "Trannies" as they were called, were all the rage. They were portable, nifty and easy to tune between different stations, whereas it was practically a criminal offence to adjust the tuning on the big valve radio on the shelf in the kitchen which the old people kept firmly tuned to Radio Éireann. However, my older brother had discovered the pirate ship broadcasts from Radio Caroline, and then Fabulous 208: Radio Luxembourg with Bob Stewart, Paul Burnett, David Christian, Kid Jensen and the Powerplay.

After Radio Luxembourg went off the air an American Bible radio station took over. I listened to the rich booming voice of a gospel preacher man saying: "I sleep good at night. You know why I sleep good at night? I sleep good at night because I have been *saved*."

As for myself, I hadn't found the Lord, I'd found Pop music. 'Sugar, Sugar' by Sakkarin. Dawn and 'Candida'. 'Nathan Jones' by the Three Degrees. 'If Not for You' by Olivia Newton John. 'How Much Love' by Leo Sayer. And the Bay City Rollers. Wow!

Pop music charted every mood, from the downer of pimples and a silent letterbox on Valentine's Day to the up-tempo rush of summer holidays. Listening to Donny Osmond convulsed by the strains of 'Puppy Love', I forgot my impossible crush on all three of *Charlie's Angels* and

Jethro's daughter in *The Beverly Hillbillies*. Even the gorgeous Lesley Anne Down was pushed from my Number One spot when I discovered Suzy Quatro. And late at night, when that Preacher came on air, I raised my voice along with him and cried, "Hallelujah, brother. I have been saved."

*

Under pressure from my older brother, Terry, my mother and father bought a PYE record player on the hire purchase. It had a reversible stylus and a 78-speed setting for the original gramophone recordings pressed in shellac. You could set the speed at 33.3 for vinyl long-playing albums, or click the speed up to 45rpm to play the free single that came with the record player. It told the story of PJ the DJ, who would spin the hits no more, having died in a car wreck at the age 24. After one listen, we spun Big Tom no more. Instead, we pooled our pocket money and sent an order off to:

McHugh Himself
39 Talbot Street,
Dublin 1.

We got all our pop records by mail order from this exotic address. McHugh Himself also stocked Irish chart music, dominated by the showbands promoted in the lurid blue and red typography of *Spotlight* magazine. We weren't as keen on the Showbands as the pop stars on Radio Luxembourg, but for cover versions Tweed were okay. And we were happy to order the latest releases from our homegrown heroes: Rory Gallagher, Phil Lynott with Thin Lizzie, and especially the Horslips.

We shared the use of the record player and rows were limited to who blunted the diamond tipped stylus or what should we play next, the Horslips' *Book of Invasions* or Neil Diamond's *Beautiful Noise*.

In December that year, Terry broke up with his girlfriend. She worked in the meat factory in Ballaghadereen and drove her own Fiat Riva. He took the break-up badly. For consolation he sent an order off to McHugh Himself. From the moment it arrived, the Mud song, 'Lonely this Christmas' went on automatic repeat play. For two weeks without let-up we heard how it would be lonely this Christmas; it would be lonely and cold. After the umpteenth play my father in desperation spirited the record away and burnt it.

Along with the mail order records from McHugh Himself, parcels began to arrive from Peats of Parnell Street in Dublin with capacitors, diodes and state-of-the-art transistors, and in Grandad's old workshop the chassis of a vale radio took on a new life.

"What is it?" I asked Terry.

"An amplifier," he said.

To demonstrate, he plugged his handiwork into the mains electricity supply. We heard a bang, followed by a shot of blue flame, followed by my father looking for wire to repair the main fuse.

The next outing for the amplifier was the parish hall. Terry had hooked up the amplifier to the record player borrowed from home. Two additional loudspeaker cabinets had been hammered together in the woodwork class in school.

The amplifier buzzed and cracked throughout Terry's first Youth Disco. But it proved both a career and technical breakthrough, especially the two homemade light boxes, each with six coloured bulbs running in sequence. And when Terry got offered a hotel gig he splashed out on a liquid-wheel projector and twin turntables to crosscut between records and intros, with his ears squashed into giant headphones.

His timing was good. As Abba won the Eurovision song contest and conquered the dance floors, ballrooms like the Mayflower experienced their own Waterloo.

The ballrooms had always been big and uncomfortable but they drew the crowd. But as the price of admission kept going up, the showbands gradually priced themselves out of the market. During the oil crises, the heating costs went through the roof, just like most of the heat, and the ballrooms grew even more cold and uninviting. And to top it all, you couldn't buy a drink.

Disco bars and hotel nightclubs with late bar exemptions grew so popular Terry needed help to carry the extra mobile disco gear. My younger brother, Dermot, joined him on the road.

"Ned Zepplin? Never heard of him." Dermot would say, having orders from Terry to ignore requests for heavy metal. More than one request for Deep Purple's 'Smoke on the Water' meant the Headbangers were in, and they'd end up having to 'pull the rig' and run for safety without getting paid.

The law kept watch.

At a 21st birthday party Terry was DJ for the night and Dermot was the helper. The rest of us were out on the floor when he guards raided the premises. Instead of clearing everyone out onto the streets at closing time, the sergeant leading the raid had his men block the exits. The sergeant then marched the crowd out the front door where he stood with his notebook open.

"The sergeant is a sour gent tonight," said the birthday girl to Terry and Dermot, who instructed her and her friends to grab a piece of disco equipment. Marching in a line, Terry approached the sergeant first, holding up a box full of records. "I was doing the music tonight," he said, claiming employee's immunity.

"Okay, you can go ahead," said the sergeant without taking his name.

The birthday girl raised a microphone stand and cable and said: "I'm with him."

"All right," the sergeant allowed her to pass.

"I'm with the disco," Dermot had a loudspeaker cabinet hoisted on one shoulder.

"Go on," the Sergeant said still without a name in his notebook.

I carried a speaker cabinet. The girl after me had a light box. Her friend was carrying another. Finally the sergeant closed his notebook and said: "Who was playing here tonight, James Last?"

The old guard could taunt, but the disco meant more than getting a crowd out on the dance floor at a 21st. Hauling us out of the backwater doldrums, pop music struck an enduring love note that proclaimed the coming of age of my generation.

THE GLOBAL VILLAGE

After the disco we squeezed into my brother Terry's canary-yellow Ford Escort with his Nite Life disco trailer hitched on the back and headed off for burgers, chips and the can of Coke.

As the fryers bubbled, country lads shoved in six deep at the counter of the late-night chipper. Lowing like suck calves for salt, grease and vinegar after the feed of pints, one voice louder than the rest roared, "Peg us out a beef burger with a ridge of onions on top."

Another man asked, "How much is a chips and nothing?"

Outside the chipper the cars had racing stripes, spoilers, spotlights and sweeping Citizen Band radio antennas.

We got our CB radios across the border in the open-air markets in Mullen. Running hot radios across the border made us feel close to the spirit of Burt Reynolds in *Smoky and the* Bandit, Kris Kristofferson, old Rubber Duck himself, in *Convoy*, and the Duke boys from Hazard County. CB radios belonged to the paraphernalia of the rebel South, like Confederate flags and musical car-horns. More than a craze, they were a totem of bandit youth.

"Breaker for a copy? Do you read me? Over."

"That's a big ten-four. What's your handle there good buddy, come back?"

We had 30 channels of free and illegal conversation. Click the dial at any hour for snatches of everyone's business.

"Did I meet you at a disco last week?"

"I don't remember."

"I remember you. You were an awful dose."

"I must have been horrid drunk."

Only channel 9 was silent. It was kept clear because it was supposed to be the emergency channel, though we had no idea what agency would respond if we broadcast a distress signal; the police, ambulance, civil defence or air-sea rescue?

If it was illegal to own a CB radio, it was doubly illegal to add heat to boost the power of the standard output. But that's what brought us to the top of the mountain later that night, my brothers Terry and Dermot and myself, and a doctored CB radio.

We parked just short of the coal mine at Rockhill. Following instructions I carried the fibreglass aerial to the top of the highest spoil heap and planted the shaft in the mountain of slate and rock from the mine.

As Terry adjusted the signal I swivelled the aerial to snare a signal. Freak atmospheric conditions could produce the most unlikely results. We already had a sizeable collection of postcards from ham radio enthusiasts we'd contacted in England, Scotland, Iceland and Denmark.

At first, the 'woodpecker' signal broke in on several channels. The woodpecker was a curious putt-putt-putt radio static sound thought to originate in Russia. Some said the signal was used to create a standing radio wave over America to disrupt military signals. Others believed it was part of an under the horizon radar system.

"Breaker for a copy," Dermot tested. "Breaker for a copy, over."

"Read it! Read it!" responded the Bullfrog.

"Get lost, will ya."

Nobody knew the culprit, but whenever two people got chatting on the CB, a repetitive "Read it… Read it" kept breaking in. It was funny at first, but soon got annoying when the Bullfrog chased you through every change of channel interrupting every conversation.

We pumped up the power, hoping to make contact with a long-haul trucker in America.

"Breaker for a copy."

"Hello there. Hamburg speaking," a voice burst from the CB loudspeaker.

"This is Ireland calling."

"Good evening Ireland."

"Read it! … Read it!" croaked the Bullfrog.

"Putt-putt-putt" went the woodpecker.

"Jaysus! It's as good as the Eurovision," said Dermot.

In the distance a siren started.

"Listen," Terry called for silence.

We searched the countryside below and spotted a string of headlights. The cavalcade was several miles away but moving in our direction.

"They couldn't be on to us that quick," Terry said.

The cavalcade kept getting nearer. And then I spotted blue lights flashing. Cop cars.

"Hello Hamburg, we have a technical problem."

"Reading you loud and clear, over?"

"Ten, ten, Hamburg. Over and out," Dermot abandoned the transmission.

"There's a fire somewhere," I said unconvinced.

"Time to pull the rig," Terry said, hurriedly disconnecting wires while I hauled down the aerial. All the time I kept expecting the speeding car headlights to veer off in another direction but each turn they took brought them closer to the source of our illicit broadcast.

"They're headed this way," I croaked.

Terry and Dermot stopped what they were doing to watch more cop cars join the chase. We were on a high and isolated mountain road. If we moved the cops would spot our car headlights, and it was too dark to drive without lights. They veered again and started up the mountain road.

"Crikey!" said Dermot and grabbed up the remaining equipment into a rough bundle.

We ran up the road and tossed the CB radio, outlawed booster, car battery, aerial and connections over the ditch. Then we crossed to the opposite ditch and got down behind the rocks. The sirens and lights were almost on top of us.

A familiar Volkswagen beetle raced past on the road below the spoil heap, so fast the driver miss-judged the turn and went into the ditch. Jets of mud sprayed from the wheels and smoke billowed from the exhaust pipe before the engine cut out. Behind it, a white squad car, a blue squad car and an unmarked Special Branch car slewed to a stop on the loose gravel. Doors thudded. We were as silent as the rock.

Uniformed figures sprinted in the flashing light towards the crashed car squarely lined up in the headlights.

"Pigs," we heard the driver of the Volkswagen roar.

"Book him, Danno," a big-bellied plainclothes detective laughed.

"Next time you're asked, you'll pull over at a check-point!" the uniformed guard said, delivering the drunk driver into the back of the squad car with a sturdy boot up the backside.

The commotion died down. The cop cars left the scene. But we waited on behind our rock, as a world of lights glimmered in the countryside below.

When we were certain the coast was clear, we gathered up the scattered radio components to resume the broadcast to our newly found pal in Hamburg. I held up the torch as Terry worked in the beam of light, reconnecting wires to the radio, battery and loudspeaker. To me it felt like we belonged to a resistance movement, but it was Terry who broke the silence.

"Back when I was going around on a bicycle done up with coloured insulating tape," he said, "the man driving that Volkswagen used to give Daddy a lift home from the pub. He had a job in the pit. He had a coal-miner's wage. He had a car. He went to the pub. He was what you might call a role model, a man of the world."

FUTURE DIRECTIONS

I had no idea where my life was headed. I read a lot but I was a chronic daydreamer. With the Leaving Certificate examinations looming I bought a red and a black biro, and an Ashling copybook with an Irish round tower printed on the cover. On the first page of the copybook I drew a neat margin the width of a schoolboy's wooden ruler. I used the red pen to draw the margin and wrote my opening remarks with a black pen – black ink had more gravity than the regular blue biro with the chewed top I used for schoolwork. Starting a diary, I hoped, would help me find a direction.

I set about writing my in private in the shed which my older brother Terry had taken over to recondition the gearbox of his second-hand Ford Escort. The workbench was loaded with cogwheels and spanners and cans of grease. Hanging from a nail on the wall, a near-naked girl posing on the STP motor-oil calendar suggested a sexy profession, but I couldn't see the glamour in stripping engines.

I liked science more. But I was living in the coal-mining valley of Arigna, where a miner's wage was tempting. Maybe I should go underground and work with a pickaxe and a navvy shovel on the Table of the Elements?

Secondary school education was free, but college cost money. Some managed to finish BAs and H.Dips. But the initials most people ended up with after their names were ESB, CIE, P&T and AIB.

In the corner of the shed where I reflected on these future career choices stood the gutted main-frame of a Marconni Marine transmitter. I hadn't the slightest interest in going to sea – "Join the Navy and see Cork harbour" was the joke at school. Both of my brothers were interested in pirate radio. And I might have followed the same career as a DJ, only their wayward pirate signal broke in on the parish priest's PA in the middle of Mass one Sunday. Suddenly my brother Dermot's voice burst over the chapel loudspeakers to announce Tom Jones and, "Why, Why, Why, Delilah?" Divine Intervention pulled the plug on another career.

There was always the option to stay put and work on the land. Every Tuesday at the local mart I could discuss export certs and headage payments, round bales, wraps and double wraps, treatments and balers. Why study a foreign language when I could learn to talk 'silage'?

I sat my exams that June and the diary was abandoned in the rafters of the shed. It never occurred to me that instead of mechanics, science, coal-mining or farming, the act of starting the diary itself gave notice of my intentions, as I drew a straight margin and thought of the words to follow

THE GLASS WOMAN

PART TWO

V

Teresa was on her way from America to see her sister Lil. She was flying into Dublin airport. Travelling on her own, she rang to say she had decided against car hire "We have enough worries," she said, "without a car smash outside Dublin airport."

My mother told her not to panic or get distracted. Lil had lost weight but she was cheerful. She was in no pain, happy to be out of the hospital and back in her own home. And the new windows would be going in any day now.

"Windows!" Teresa said. "What in God's name is she thinking?"

"It's what she wants," my mother said. She put down the phone then to prepare for the visit.

Like my mother and Lil, Teresa was another widow. Her late husband, Pat Donnelly, had relatives in the North, but for the most part Teresa would be spending her fortnight in Ireland with my mother. Seeing Lil was the chief purpose of the visit, but Teresa would probably like to meet a few people around home. If Teresa had no car hired, it might be easier to invite these friends and relations to meet her instead of spending days motoring Teresa around to see them separately. So the idea of a family get-together was back on the agenda.

If a gathering was to be organised to welcome Teresa to Ireland, I felt we might as well use the opportunity to celebrate the twin's 70th birthday. It would also take pressure off my mother, who would be entertaining Teresa over the coming two weeks. As for Lil, a party in her honour might be no substitute for a clean bill of health, but her feisty response to her condition was heartening and the occasion might further boost her spirits.

At the same time I wanted to do what was best for Lil. The twins were a hardy strain and Lil had made a great recovery. But that didn't change what the doctor had said: Lil had advanced cancer of the spine. And Lil had this constant worry that sudden stress or exertion might cause a bone in her back to snap without warning, leaving her paralysed. Was it asking too much to expect her to attend a party and cope with even a small crowd of well wishers?

If I had to abandon the notion of an actual birthday party for my mother and her twin sister, I was determined to make Teresa feel welcome. I had fond memories of gatherings in the past when Teresa's husband, Pat Donnelly, my father Matt, and Lil's husband, John Beirne, were alive and the Americans came home on holiday. The influence these gatherings had on my life went deep, deeper maybe than I had appreciated until now when it seemed my turn to keep the tradition alive.

I had watched countless hours of American television over the years. So I knew exactly what the grownups meant when they said that my mother's cousin from America reminded them of Phil Silvers in *Sergeant Bilko*. Or that there was a striking likeness between a visiting American aunt and Lucille Ball in *I Love Lucy*. From the Christmas re-runs of *King Kong* on the television every year, or from pouring over the family photo album at home, I was more familiar with the Manhattan skyline and the Empire State Building than any streetscape or building in Dublin. The coins the Americans offloaded once they arrived in Ireland allowed me to grasp real nickels, dimes and quarters and the meaning of 'two-bit punks' who got a slap in the face from Humphrey Bogart.

My imagination was furnished wholesale with Hollywood and syndicated TV Americana. And when my aunts and uncles and cousins came home on holiday they brought the authentic flavours and rewards of America to our family table.

My idea of luxury food at the time was Chef Salad Cream or a jar of Heinz Sandwich Spread. But the Americans imported all kinds of bribes into the daily meals at home to help my cousins adjust. I relished exotic meatball and spaghetti suppers, Philadelphia cream cheese and Jelly sandwiches, Ritz crackers, peanut butter, Hellmann's Real Mayonnaise. For breakfast I was supposed to eat porridge oat flakes, but despite the constant warnings from my mother, I couldn't keep my hands off the visitors' stash of cornflakes and rice krispies. And the 'sodas' that arrived in our house by the caseload turned out to be 'the real thing,' in authentic corrugated-glass Coca Cola bottles.

In return for the American treats the visitors got big Irish fried breakfasts every morning with chunky rashers and sausages bursting out of their skins, country eggs, black pudding and white pudding and freshly baked soda bread. After a 'tightener' of a breakfast, and 'full as a tic', the Americans headed off for the day. When they arrived back they had bought leg of lamb for the dinner and it wasn't even Sunday.

Before the family sat down to eat the roast leg of lamb my mother warned my brothers and me to go easy. Only the visitors were allowed second helpings. So when my mother put the question, "Anyone for more meat?" we repeated in turn the answer drummed into us, "No thanks, Mammy… No thanks, Mammy… No thanks, mammy…"

Every night a party started in the kitchen at home. Cartons of soft pack, duty-free Kent cigarettes were passed around and in the scullery the men in private toasts raised their duty-free whisky in American shot glasses. Neighbours called around and got welcomed in with more duty-free drink. The stay-at-home girls with plain faces, bad teeth and straight hair squeezed their Hohner accordions and played, 'The Hag with the Money' and 'The Rose in the Heather'.

We could do little to compensate the visitors for their generosity. But Irish pub ashtrays were prized souvenirs in America, especially the big glazed ashtrays that advertised Powers or Jameson Irish whiskey. When they came home on holiday the Americans were determined to bag at least one ashtray on every visit. It was a duty and an adventure to accommodate them.

One time, Pat Donnelly, Teresa's husband, went trophy hunting with my father. As the ashtrays in the local bar were battered and shabby, my father suggested they drive further afield in the hired car. They stopped at a pub in town with a new 'singing lounge' extension built onto the back. There my father told the owner he had a bit of business he wanted to discuss with the Yank in private.

Expecting a windfall, the owner opened up the singing lounge.

The instant they were alone, my father pointed to the rows of tables, each with a spotless new ashtray, and said to Uncle Pat: "Take your pick."

The story of how he came by the ashtray was as important to Uncle Pat as the souvenir. It reinforced his belief in his own and his compatriot's uniqueness.

"The women will be all right," my father would say to Uncle Pat, signalling that while my mother, Lil and Aunt Teresa went off for the day, shopping and sightseeing, they were headed for the pub.

In the pub they spent the day swapping yarns that celebrated the skewed and exceptional outlook of the Irish: a great favourite being Eamonn Kelly's yarn about the Irish level-crossing with one gate open and one gate closed. "What's going on?" the tourist asked. To which the gatekeeper said: "We're half-expecting a train."

With the drinks bought and his change left beside his elbow on the bar counter, Uncle Pat would continue with the story about 'the guy from home', who went to Dublin to collect an American relative at the airport. On the way home from the airport he drove the wrong way down several one-way streets, but his passenger from America didn't seem to notice. They got home and stopped at the local pub. The place was quiet. The men at the bar gave them a sullen glance, looking out from under their eyebrows before turning back to their pints. The silence continued until the American said, "Beats me. In Dublin, the cars are flashing their lights and everybody waves at you. While here at home nobody knows - or talks - to you."

Like the bar in the story, the bar where Uncle Pat and my father drank had that murky light slanting in the windows and the same unbanishable gloom in the corners, a haze of blue smoke in the air from the company of men at the bar on their second or third pint by mid-morning.

Ranged along the bar were the real people who populated the pub stories. Characters like Denny, who was in the pub one evening when a neighbour ran in to say Denny's cattle had broken into the meadow field and were tramping Denny's crop of hay into the ground. Denny raised a fresh pint and said: "They'll be sorry next winter."

Denny's lifelong companion at the bar was his neighbour Frank; a man who spent so much time sitting on a high stool at the end of the bar with his back to the wall that the track of his head had worn in the wallpaper.

Frank had a cow stuck in a drain one time. He asked Denny for help.

'Is she in far?' Denny asked.

'Up to her ankles,' Frank said.

'Could you not run her out?'

'She's upside down.'

As Uncle Pat sat there, enjoying the yarns and buying pints and chasers for the bachelors, the subsidy farmers and the men three days on the beer, he would shake his head from time to time and remark with the gratitude of a man holding a return ticket, "Only for America, I'd be just like those guys on the high stool every day."

In those days, transatlantic travel really was a novelty and a privilege - even if it often meant a lifetime lived in exile. Nowadays Disneyland in Florida was a popular Irish family holiday destination. Glossy magazines promoted the idea of weekend shopping trips from Dublin to New York. Highfliers in the technology and business sectors regarded the constant trips between America and Ireland as 'more pressure'. Even on holiday visits, hectic lifestyles make it awkward for Irish and American cousins to meet and greet or entertain each other when visiting their respective countries, if they even bother to keep in touch. International arrivals and departures were prone to pass without a sense of occasion, significance or ceremony. And that was the essential reason I wanted this party for Teresa, Lil and my mother, and their oldest friends and relations. In the knowledge that there might not be anything like it again, the party represented a wishful return to happier times.

*

A surprise party would be ludicrous, so I told my mother straight out what I was planning.

"I have lettuce in the garden," my mother said. "So don't go buying anything."

I took this to be her way of saying yes.

But with only a week to go to the actual birthday I kept putting off calling the other guests. Lil was frail. And I suspected she was losing ground.

I decided to telephone my sister-in-law Josephine for her advice. Married to my older brother Terry, I find her kind, fearless and direct and I trust her judgement. Josephine and Terry also lived near both twins and Lil would cycle past their house twice a day on her way to and from her job picking mushrooms. Josephine had grown very fond of Lil who got into the habit of stopping sometimes for a chat. Josephine also took my mother shopping and elsewhere when she needed a lift, and they got on well. She seemed the best-placed to give impartial direction, and she listened carefully when I told her about the intended party for the two birthday girls. A party that would include their sisters, Aunt Teresa from America and Aunt Kathleen from County Meath, who would be meet Teresa at Dublin airport and bring her to see Lil as soon as Teresa was up to the next leg of the journey west. Along with the immediate family, five others would be invited to the party – all of them good friends and related in some way through blood or marriage to my mother and Lil.

I barely had time to finish outlining the plan before Josephine said she'd be delighted to help out with the arrangements. And straight away she volunteered to contribute to the grocery bill.

"I don't want to impose," I said.

"I'd like to do it," she said. "Especially for Lil and your mother. And Teresa was very good to Terry and myself when we were in America with the children last year."

She also offered to host the party. She had extra bedrooms to put up anyone who wanted to stay overnight. And her house was between Lil's house and my mother's home place so Lil would not have to travel far for the party.

"Great idea," I said.

"As long as you're sure you want to go through with this?" she said, gently letting me know she fully supported the notion but had doubts about the practicalities. I told her I had weighed up the pros and cons and believed the party should go ahead.

"That's fine," she said.

Putting down the phone I hoped I sounded confident.

A day later Josephine rang back. She had news. She said the new windows had arrived and Lil was ready to stay with my mother while the windows went in. If we moved the party to my mother's house it would suit Lil. She could rest before the party, meet everyone and go to bed early without making a fuss if she felt tired.

This development was the prompt I needed and I set about

calling my mother's friends one after the other with the invitations. These phone calls followed a pattern. The first question inevitably: "How is Lil?"

"She's at home," I said. "But it is cancer she has. It's in the spine and we just have to wait and see."

"And your mother?"

"She's upset but she keeps going. She's 70 this week"

"That's right"

"We're expecting Teresa from America. Can you come over?"

"Is it a party?"

"More of a get-together."

"Like the old times."

"Exactly."

VI

We were homebirds at heart. My older brother, Terry, lived a short distance from the home place. My younger brother, Dermot, was also married and lived away from the home place with his wife Margaret and two children, but he spent a lot of time working on the farm on the mountain. And I lived only a half-hour drive from Crosshill. Even though we lived within a short radius of each other we did not often meet. If needs be, it was understood, a call for help would bring us together immediately.

While we three brothers seldom met socially, our wives had to improvise friendships around our occasional get-togethers. Still the party arrangements were working out exceptionally straightforward. With the cooperation of all sides the cost of the food and the drink and the share of responsibilities had been delegated down to the place and the cutlery settings, prompting my brother Dermot to remark, "It's good to see a family take out the forks along with the knives."

Aunt Kathleen rang from her home to confirm everything had gone well at Dublin airport and Teresa was now resting. Tomorrow they would set out from Meath with Kathleen's husband, Pat Tuite, doing the driving.

Now retired, Kathleen and Pat had lived in America for many years, before returning to Ireland to run a business and to bring up a young family. When Teresa had a heart bypass operation two summers before, Kathleen flew to New York and went directly to Long Island to help Teresa convalesce. And when Lil had to have an operation for breast cancer, Kathleen made constant visits to the hospital to see her. Kathleen was thoughtful, level-headed, yet impulsive when she had good cause to be impulsive. She was probably the best all round at coping with upsets in the family.

It felt good to be bringing these women together again despite the shadow of cancer darkening the family occasion. And I was glad the family had stuck to their guns and gone ahead with the party.

On the morning itself, I had little to do beyond boiling a saucepan full of potatoes to make potato salad. But I rang Josephine to find out if there were any last minute jobs that might have been overlooked.

When I got no reply at home I tried her mobile number.

"Hold on," she answered. "I can't talk here."

Back again on the line a minute or so later her voice sounded odd.

"Where are you?" I asked.

"I'm at the hospital," she said.

"What happened?"

"Lil had a fall."

"O God! How is she?"

"Bad. They say the bone went in her hip."

I quailed at the news. Lil's worst nightmare had come true - a bone snapping suddenly, causing loss of mobility and hospital admission.

According to Josephine the doctors believed the break happened as a result of the fall. But I wondered out loud if weakened by cancer the bone had broken and caused her to fall.

"I hadn't thought of that," Josephine said.

"When did it happen?" I asked.

"This morning," Josephine said. "I called around to see if she wanted anything from town ahead of the party. When I got to the house Sean had her back in the chair but Lil was in agony. We loaded her into my car and I drove her to the hospital. She was in a bad way."

"She must have got an awful fright." I said.

"When they admitted her," Josephine said, "the nurses told me she was in shock."

*

After Kathleen got news of Lil's fall she rang to say she and Teresa were driving straight to the hospital. I told Kathleen I had just got back from the hospital where I found Lil asleep, probably sedated. I didn't want to disturb Lil. Instead I spoke to one of the nurses.

"What did the nurse say?" Kathleen asked.

It was time to stop downplaying the seriousness of Lil's condition. "It's not good," I said.

I heard Aunt Kathleen's breath catch before she said, "But she was fine the last time I saw her."

"She's lost a lot of ground since then," I said. "You're going to get a shock. And so is Teresa."

In the early evening I arrived at the home place with food and drink prepared for the party. I met Josephine who was unloading more food from her car. Together we gathered up the bowls and plates full of what appeared now an unseemly amount of food. I said I wanted to ring people and tell them not to come. My first priority was to get my mother to the hospital. There she could meet her sisters and together they could talk to Lil and comfort her.

"Talk to your mother first," Josephine said.

My mother met us at the front door. Pale and subdued, she was anxious that we leave the food in the scullery where it would stay cool. I said as soon as I had the car emptied I was ready to turn around and drive her to the hospital.

My mother stalled. She said we couldn't turn people away at the eleventh hour. And she couldn't leave the house with Teresa and Kathleen coming to stay and their closest friends coming to see them.

"They'll understand," I said.

"I can't leave," she insisted.

Clearly she did not want to go to the hospital and it dawned on me she was unable to face her twin sister.

"Anyway, when they get back from the hospital Teresa and Kathleen will have to eat," Josephine said.

"But will they want to entertain visitors?" I said.

"It might be better if they have company," Josephine said.

My mother retreated from the scullery and found a job to do upstairs. I looked at Josephine. She lowered her voice and said, "Teresa and Kathleen are being told."

"But they know."

"No one has said it straight out to them."

"And now they're on the way back here to a party?"

*

We arranged the plates on top of the sideboard in the kitchen to allow people to help themselves to the food. To make more space on the sideboard I removed a pair of matching plaster cast cocker spaniels, an ornamental oil lamp and other trinkets while my mother hovered uneasily.

She was upset with this displacement of familiar things.

We pressed ahead.

In every circumstance but one, the home place was now perfect for the party. My mother had the fire in the kitchen built up and the house was cosy and neat with embroidered cloths on the small table where the drink was arranged: a selection of red and white wine, whiskey, and beer. The cushions on the chairs in the kitchen had clean covers and the armchairs and settee in the sitting room had matching lace covers on the armrests and along the back. The kettle on the hob was steaming, another electric kettle was set to boil at the flick of a plastic switch, and the teapot with the lid off was ready for scalding and the tea caddy to hand. The willow pattern teacups and saucers had been taken out of the press and were stacked on a tray in the scullery with the milk jug and sugar bowl. I was worried we mightn't have enough strong drink but my mother put the greater emphasis on tea.

As we worked I kept listening until I finally heard the car pull up outside. I went directly to meet Teresa and Kathleen.

The evening was dry but cloudy and I approached them in the dwindling light. Both women were red-eyed and tearful with tissues crushed in their fists.

I met Teresa first and hugged her. "How are you?" I said.

"O now!" she said.

I patted her on the back.

"You tried to warn us," Kathleen said.

"There's tea inside," I said.

My mother met her two sisters in the hallway. She kept back from Teresa and Kathleen a pace or two but her first words were, "Poor Lil. What happened at all? She was doing so well."

The tears sprang from Teresa and Kathleen's eyes. And while the sisters gathered in the kitchen I went to the scullery with the boiling kettle. Josephine was already there, righting the teacups in their saucers.

"Your mother is great," she said.

"She has no choice," I said. "She has all these people coming. I should have heeded you more."

"Look," said Josephine. "They're as well-off entertaining people. If they were here on their own they'd spend the night crying and bickering over what more could have been done for Lil."

The first guest to show up was Paddy Joe Conlon. I shook his hand warmly, feeling especially glad to see him. Paddy Joe was a tactful man with a great sense of humour. If any man could strike a balance between a sense of occasion and loss it was Paddy Joe.

He had arrived with his daughter, Mary, and he apologised on behalf of his wife, Molly, who couldn't make it. Kathleen Daly arrived next with a shopping bag loaded with sweet cake and whiskey. She was a first cousin of the sisters and another widow. Kathleen was an exceptionally generous and exceptionally shy person, who had shared a table with my mother and Lil at the evening party after I got married to Carmel. Whenever anyone belonging to Carmel approached their table and spoke to Kathleen, my mother or Lil answered on her behalf. Nobody recalled Kathleen getting a word in the whole night.

The remaining cousin, Peter and his wife Margaret arrived and the supper was served immediately out of a need for something to keep the evening going.

It was a difficult situation for everyone, knowing that Lil was in the hospital and her condition was now openly acknowledged as terminal. But at least people were hungry. The platters of food on the sideboard were cleared and the potato salad was popular. By this stage the scullery had also filled up with a mysterious amount of cakes and extra-large bottles of whiskey in gift boxes.

I went around with second helpings and more tea. The food, together with the tea, the drinks on arrival and the consolation of friends lifted our spirits.

"Any sign of Sean?" Teresa asked.

"I've saved a plate of food for him and Dermot," my mother said. "The forecast is good and they've rigged extra lights on the tractor to go mowing the last of the hay."

"It's like this," Dermot said, grabbing a sandwich on his own way to the hayfield. "He's better off working at the hay. A party without Lil is too much like a wake."

Aunt Teresa looked to be on the brink of delivering a piece of her mind. But it didn't happen. She held back. And I thought: it's when you expect the worst that people are often strongest.

Feeling it was safe to lift her eyes from the plate, Aunt Kathleen said "Lord, do you remember the fuss Grandad made cutting the hay?"

"He was a great man putting an edge on a scythe," Paddy Joe gallantly took up the conversation. "You'd spin twice and fall over if you swung the blade too hard."

"The sign of a good edge on a blade," my mother said, "is when you can shave the hair off the back of a mouse sleeping in the field without waking it up."

"That's very good," Teresa smiled.

"It was Monica Carr, I think, that said that," my mother said.

"And then Grandad would cycle to Bundoran when the hay was saved," said Kathleen, "for a day by the sea."

"It was a long way to go just to paddle your feet," said Peter's wife Margaret.

"He'd cycle there and back the same day," Teresa said.

"We thought nothing about cycling then," my mother said.

The others around the table fell silent and Kathleen Daly bowed her head.

One of the hardest things to endure in life is how often the kindest are dealt the cruellest blows. And into my mind came that picture of Lil cycling her bike into the village of Keadue day in and day out.

"The poor soul," my mother sighed under her breath.

Paddy Joe said, "Do you mind the time Kate the Miller fell off her bike outside Arigna chapel. She was speechless and the bike was spokeless. And she never let up about her accident until she heard your father Henry Joe telling the priest, 'To hear the way she goes on you'd swear she fell out of an aeroplane.'"

More tea and more stories followed. But out of respect for what the family had been through that day there was a general move to leave on time. When the party broke up it was not late by the standards of the past and everyone left together.

After the house cleared we plugged in the electric kettle for a last cup of tea. Then we gathered in the lower room, looking into the embers of the fire.

"Thank you," Teresa said turning to everyone involved. "We had a good night after all."

"We haven't had anything like it in years," said Aunt Kathleen. But her voice trailed off and we knew precisely what was left unspoken - "If only Lil could have been with us."

My mother looked pale and shaken and Kathleen asked, "Are you all right, Nan?"

"It's frightening," my mother said, "how easy it is to lose touch with all belonging you."

REDUNDANCIES

FAMINE WALLS AND RIBBON CODES

Ireland experienced an economic boom throughout the 1980s. Huge numbers of young people applied for holiday visas. Their applications to the American Embassy in Dublin revealed every one of them had personal savings and a job, sometimes two jobs. It would be a glorious Irish joke only for the desperation, the heartbroken families, and the haemorrhage of talented, young, go-ahead people from a country that could offer them nothing only the lies they needed to escape.

Apart from the birth certificates and passports, the bulk of the testimonials carried by the visa applicants were bogus: fake evidence of fake jobs, fake money in fake accounts, and fake promises to return to fake places of employment after the fake holiday: a litany of misinformation, duplicity and falsehood on a Grotesque, Unprecedented, Bizarre and Unbelievable scale. And an Irish Foreign Minister, Brian Lenihan, who said: "We can't all live on a small island."

On one side of the security barriers outside the American Embassy in Dublin you had the Anti-American protestors holding candlelight vigils after the invasion of Grenada, volunteer coffee pickers who backed the Sandinistas, or supporters of Yasser Arafat and the people of Palestine. While on the other side stood the line of young people from all over Ireland with their heads down, queuing quietly in line for visas.

Around the home place the dark angel of emigration passed over every household. Even at the weekends the town of Drumshanbo was like a cemetery with lights on. Across the countryside, sons, daughters, entire

171

families were compelled to uproot in search of employment. Owners who could no longer meet the savage rates of interest repayment on their mortgages abandoned newly built houses. People left overnight, depositing house keys through the letterbox of the bank or the building society. As one man said to me: "If you owe the bank £500, that's your problem. If you owe the bank £50,000, that's their problem."

Anger and the urge to bear witness, stung me into writing about what was happening. I submitted an article to the *Leitrim Observer*, comparing the walls built around the big estates by the starving tenants during the Great Famine with the walls being built by the unemployed on government social employment schemes. Amazingly, the editor of the *Leitrim Observer* accepted and published the piece. And very soon afterwards I got an official letter stating that I was technically unemployed and therefore available for work on a Social Employment Scheme. The letter gave me an ultimatum: either sign off the dole or report on Monday for building duty on the great wall of FAS.

It seemed a good time to join that line of suspiciously down-at-heel holidaymakers outside the American Embassy. As a final act of leave-taking I decided to take the dog for a long walk on the mountain.

Our dog, Sally, had been knocked down by a car years before, but she survived to accompany me whenever I went walking. If she got tired walking she lifted her bad leg and skipped along after me, prompting my father to say she reminded him of an abacus where you carry one and bring three.

A line of mature beech trees distinguished the farm on the mountain, and in the embankment under the beech trees there appeared to be a traditional sweathouse. Before my time, these field-stone sweathouses had been built into clay embankments and used as primitive saunas and steam cures for tuberculosis; you lit a fire inside to heat a pile of stones and when the fire burnt out you splashed water on the hot stones to bathe in the steam inside the sweathouse. Locating these relics of the past often gave a direction and a goal to my walks.

The field-stone monument on the farm on the mountain was unusual in that it had two chambers. In fact, this structure was a smokehouse, an adaptation of an idea that, like the beech trees, must have been borrowed from his landlord by a local land agent with notions of importance. Getting down on my hands and knees, I was able to crawl into the larger of the two chambers. Here, joints of raw meat once hung from the ceiling. A fire was then lit in the smaller cell and a crosscurrent of smoke passed through the connecting passage to cure the meat.

The smokehouse was my first stop that evening. After I left it and the beech trees I hiked up the fields, following the sheep-paths through the dips and hollows where stones had been quarried in earlier days and Sally now yelped and ambled after the rabbits using the gorse bushes for cover.

The evening was damp and murky, but I walked on as far as a stone cabin or a 'bothy' on the side of the mountain, built where the fields ended and the heather and rock began. The roof was missing but the lintel stone over the door stood firm. Inside, I found three small rooms. Water trickled down the lichen-covered walls. The atmosphere was sombre and a feeling of fret and gloom swelled as I moved from one cramped room to the next. In the final room there was not even a window. I did not need to know the precise history to recognise this was the property of a family near the bottom of that social order of landlord, land agent and tenant.

As I lingered in the furthest room I felt the ghost of something old and forlorn reach out and touch me, like the breath of an unseen stranger on the back of my neck. Sally looked subdued and uneasy but it was not fear I felt, more a sudden and profound sympathy with the currents of strong emotion that must have passed through this household as its tenants fought for survival in the worst of circumstances.

The rain-clouds cleared then, and the evening sunlight began to cast long shadows. In the slanted light I noticed the corrugated rows of famine ridges in the mountain pasture; the track of potato crops abandoned in plots of ground so deprived the earth had never been turned back. And seeing history surface so dramatically before my eyes brought to mind the suffering and the bitter campaigns fought for possession of these fields. I did not know the exact story, but where the facts became garbled my imagination took over.

*

1886, and times were hard in Arigna. In April, a local man, Philip Coggins, together with his ailing sister and his crippled brother, 'all looking starved' were evicted by the Countess of Kingston and her agent, Jack Tatlow. Brigid Lee, whose husband had gone to America, was also evicted along with her five children. Thomas McManus, his wife and 85-year-old mother were put out, as were Charlie Ward and his wife and six daughters. When the evictions were complete, three emergency men and a constable took up position at each cabin to prevent the tenants from returning.

The Member for Parliament, Wilfred Scawen Blunt, observed these heartless evictions. His observations were published in the *Pall Mall Gazette* in London. The case became widely debated and the matter raised in Westminster. Despite this attention, a further 53 eviction notices were served.

In December the bailiffs returned. This time, a crowd gathered and began to taunt and shout at the land agent, Jack Tatlow, his bailiffs, and his emergency men. Sticks were raised to block the land agent's path.

"The bullock for the road, the land for the people," the crowd heckled.

Tatlow turned to the Resident Magistrate and ordered him to take control of the situation. Reluctantly, the Magistrate instructed his force of over twenty police to draw batons and disperse the crowd.

They cleared a path to the door and Tatlow ordered five sisters and their 80-year-old father to evacuate the house. The old man lay dying and unable to rise. He had to be laid out on a door and carried to a neighbouring cabin. After the few sticks of furniture belonging to the family were removed, Tatlow gave the order for their home to be demolished. While the crowd stood and watched, the stones were ripped from the walls and scattered. At the sound of the roof collapsing, the crowd rushed forward and began to pelt the land agent with the fallen stones.

Tatlow and his men retreated across a dry drain towards higher ground. There the police fixed bayonets and formed a circle

Father Reddy, the parish priest, had been sent for to give extreme unction to the dying man in the neighbouring cabin. When he arrived he found the land agent, the police and the locals face-to-face and ready for bloodshed.

Father Reddy addressed the crowd.

"There is no doubt you were driven to desperation," he spoke firmly but reasonably. "But you are spoiling the cause we are fighting for. These things are hard to endure, but our aims will not be achieved by force. In the name of God, I beg you to disperse."

*

The cause they were fighting for went back a long way. From 1800 onwards the income from tillage farming on the big estates had seriously dwindled. Hundreds of small plots were cleared to make way for more economical large-scale pastures for rearing beef herds. The labourers and the smallholders were no longer wanted, left without work or an income to pay for their mud cabins and potato grounds. To put a stop to these clearances they banded into secret societies.

In canvas tents and the smoky back rooms of public houses able bodied men gathered to whisper passwords, trade nicknames and secret signs. Every district had its own secret society. Some were known as The Hearts of Steel. Others were called The White Boys. More were named by their activities: the Threshers scattered crops, the Carders tore the skin from the breast and back of their victims with the tool used for carding wool. Houghers maimed animals. About this district you had the Terry Alts from the mountain, the Peep-O'-Day-Boys and the Molly Maguires amongst the coal miners.

Such societies aimed to control unfair rents and leases, to oppose evictions and wholesale clearances, and block all bidding on lands from which labourers and tenant farmers had been evicted. The clergy, too, had their orders to fix their price for a baptism, a mass or a marriage. Publicans were also warned not to charge more than four pennies for a noggin of whiskey.

On frosty nights the Molly Maguires might be glimpsed carrying their pikestaffs and stout blackthorn sticks as they walked by the light of the poacher's moon. To confuse and terrify their victims the men wore white shirts outside their clothes, women's scarves and shawls over their heads, white bands in their hats and coloured ribbons tied to their arms. Dressed as hags, angry, secretive and oath-bound men knocked on windows, scattered harvests, burnt haystacks.

Speaking of his tenants in Ballinamuck in County Longford, Lord Lorton pronounced from his seat at Rockingham: "In consequence of finding such a bad spirit among them, I came to the determination to level the village."

These clearances were followed by the onset of the Famine.

The people blamed faulty seed for the increase in crop failures in the district, and not the fungus spores of an airborne blight. And there had been food and money shortages before, which the people endured. A wage of seven pennies a day could save a family from starvation. But now they were told the funds for public work had run dry. All work on drainage schemes and road building was suspended.

Meals were reduced to cabbage leaves, turnip tops and thinnings. Soup kitchens were set up with half-penny voucher entitlements for those working on the stone walls around the bigger estates. Most had not the money to buy the Indian corn and 'hard tack' biscuits released from army stores.

Somehow the population weathered through that first winter of crop failures. And when the blossom appeared again on the hawthorn, and gentle primrose flowers filled the sun-warmed ditches, things were thought to be on the mend. In July the potato crop flowered. "The district wears a better look," said one witness. And at the August race meeting the equipages were 'many and splendid'. But the following week brought warm fogs and shrouds of heavy air scented with corruption. A stale and faintly sweet breath of mildew lingered over the potatoes in the ground. By the end of that clammy August week of 1846 every field of stalks in the barony was black.

"Not one has married here since the potato failed," remarked one observer as entire families surrender their belongings and trudged to the workhouse for oatmeal gruel. But then workhouse doors were shut. The dispossessed were numbered in thousands. And the land clearances accelerated as the absence of tenants gave the ailing estates a better chance of economic survival.

The famine spread. The promised wheat and barley seed-corn for planting never arrived. The potato crop failed again. Nameless dead lay by the roadside with blades of grass between their teeth. A woman had to carry the body of her dead brother on her back to the graveyard. Soon the bodies had to be covered where they fell or transported in large numbers by cart and bier to anonymous famine graves opened in the frozen winter earth. With the thaw a fever began to take the more willing volunteers. The last reports from the district read: "They die like rotten sheep." As one official shortly before the complete breakdown of local administration wrote: "I have no words to paint this scene."

The names of those who died or fled the district at the height of the famine were not recorded. Entire families vanished. But through their half-acre plots of ground their names were remembered in the locality: Kiernan's lane, Doyle's acre, Patsy's garden.

The remaining families moved to higher ground, settling on mountain commonage where the heather sprouted and the rock began. People felt the blight wouldn't attack 'above the briar line'. They dug into the hillsides, built stone cabins in sheltered hollows where mountain streams ran, and lived on thin pickings: bilberry fruits, blackberries and wild birds caught on the branch with a sticky compound called birdlime, made from holly tree bark.

They hid their white ribbons and pikestaffs between the rocks and bent their backs to their turf-banks. A community of survivors. Hard as the mountain rock with deep memories and history under their feet.

*

Through the intervention of Father Reddy, Jack Tatlow and his emergency men were allowed safe passage from the mountain on that decisive December morning. The crowd jeered and hooted as the bailiffs retreated and immediately went to work re-building the fallen cabin.

"We will not be oppressed by buckshot and tyranny," they called after the land agent.

In the wake of this protest, Thomas McDermot and 11 other people were summoned by the District Inspector to appear at Ballyfarnon Petty Sessions. They were charged with being riotously, tumultuously and unlawfully assembled, making unlawful threats and endangering the public peace of Our Lady the Queen.

One woman brought before the Magistrate was threatened with a month of hard labour.

"Hard labour or soft labour, it's all the same to me," she said. "I'm well able to work."

Her attitude won a cheer from the crowd. And in a verdict that surprised many onlookers the accused that day were bound to the peace and released.

A fife and drum band and a torchlight procession welcomed the other agitators home. Rush candles glimmered in the doorways of even the poorest cabin. A turf-fire beacon burned on the summit. Thomas

McDermot announced his intention to marry his sweetheart, Ann Maria Malone.

On their wedding night Thomas warned Maria, "Our children are bound to be outlaws."

"They'll improve or finish in prison," Maria said.

*

After the formation of the Land League in 1879 a longing grew in the people for big gatherings; a need for drinking and cheering and flag-waving dormant since the Famine spread throughout the countryside. Anna Parnell, the wife of Charles Stewart Parnell, visited Keadue in March 1881 to establish a branch of the newly founded Ladies Land League. The increasing number of Land League monster meetings and demonstrations in the district prompted Ann Maria McDermot and the other women to make banners and uniforms for the horsemen who showed up now at every gathering. Using the meanest rags they revived a lost delight in show and colour and occasion.

The objectives of the Land League rallies were a continuation of the pre-famine Ribbon code: never to lease a farm from which another tenant had been evicted and to withhold rents and declare a public ban on labouring, herding or trading with anyone who broke the code. While the Land League chose peaceful means of protest, there were enough Ribbonmen and oath-bound Molly Maguires around to punish anyone who broke ranks with the League or a boycott. After the fall of night, windows were smashed. A land agent was stripped and beaten. A pistol shot finished a troublesome bailiff's life.

When lands belonging to the Kilronan estate were declared vacant, bidders from outside the district were warned off by a notice from, 'Rory of the Hills', which said, 'shoneen land-grabbers and rent-office flunkeys', would pay for their treachery if they bid against the rightful tenants.

At an auction held in Ballyfarnon courthouse the police were unable to arrest the hecklers for fear of a riot. The plan to put through the sale of an estate in one lot had to be called off; no one dared put in a bid. The lands were broken into smaller lots, which were knocked down to the tenant farmers.

The Land Leaguers had won a victory of sorts. The danger of rent arrears and evictions had eased, and after a succession of Land Acts, the introduction of a Government grant allowed tenants to buy out their smallholdings from the Congested Districts Board. The McDermot family finally took possession of their house and land with a government loan, repayable at four-and-a-half percent over forty-five years.

*

The pattern of those hard-fought land divisions had started to fade as the sun sank in the West. Sally sat watching and waiting for me to move on. But I pressed my hand against the rough wall of the stone cabin where I stood, as if I might somehow feel the passions that once ran so high about this place. Passions transmitted through a people who understood the worth of every field and stone wall, every hedgerow division, every gap and gully, every slope and hollow, every root and ribbon of grass. Standing there, I decided I could labour on walls if I had to. Eat dust all day to eat my dinner at night. Whatever it took to hold my ground.

COMFORT ALL YE SHEEPMEN

1986, and times were hard in Arigna. "I've had complaints," the parish priest read out the local sheepmen from the altar. "The flowers and the fresh wreaths in the graveyard have been eaten. Last week I discovered a number of sheep with purple markings around their necks in the front porch of the chapel, digesting the bishop's pastoral letter. I would remind you that when the bishop set his thoughts on paper he had a different flock in mind."

"He might as well save his breath to cool his porridge," my mother whispered to me with a sidelong glance at the sheepmen. "If you gave them fellas the keys to the church they'd find another use for the chalice."

One Sunday after mass, when American astronauts were racing around on moon buggies, loading up moon rock, the men standing outside the Arigna chapel wondered out loud would they ever find life up there?

"There's no grass on the moon anyway," said Tom Lavin. "Or these men I know would have sheep on it long ago."

Now the sheep were everywhere but the moon. And the sheepmen kneeled on their caps at the back of the chapel, chatting amongst themselves and paying no heed to 'His Nibs' on the altar. "I'll tell you my sins, Father," was their attitude, "but not my business."

A lot of the pitmen had turned to sheep rearing on hill farms so wet you didn't measure the land by the acre so much as you measured it by the gallon. They allowed their sheep to wander the mountain freely, where the sheep found grazing and dry places to rest along the sides of the road. Other sheepmen grazed their flocks in the forestry service plantations. To avoid being caught by the forestry officials they used binoculars to count their sheep at a safe distance, earning the name, the 'spy-glass farmers'. Others allowed their sheep to trespass on farms where the owners were either absent or unwilling to get into a row with these sheep barons. Sullen and forceful men who ruled over a kingdom of fallen stone cabins, scrap cars, misted conifer plantations, and mountains so overgrazed the heather had died, causing the peat to be washed down to bare rock.

The environmentalists and animal-rights people cried halt, seeing a catastrophe in the making. But the sheepmen had long and bitter memories going back to the official reports from Famine times when it was the tenant farmers on the mountain who were said to 'die like rotten sheep'.

Furthermore, farming had become a numbers game for sheepmen throughout the country, intent on collecting whatever grants and subsidies were available for as long as the European common agricultural policies continued and the meat plants controlled the prices. Sheep flocks were inspected by a department official, the ears punched, and the cheque collected. In some cases then, the ears were doctored and the sheep moved to another farm and a further payment collected. Some sheepmen were so expert at doctoring punch holes one onlooker remarked: "As plastic surgeons, they'd have made a fortune in Hollywood." There was also a story going around about a sheepman who spent so much time moving animals around at night he fell asleep during mass. He started to snore. To wake him up the priest raised his voice.

"Lord grant us peace." The priest raised his voice, but the sheepman snored on regardless. "Lord grant us peace," the priest repeated more loudly, causing the sheepman to jump up in his seat. "Grant!" he said. "Did someone mention a grant?"

The mass in Arigna chapel ended and the sheepmen took up their usual position outside the church porch for a smoke and a chat. A blustery shower swept down the valley, just as the met office weather forecast came over a car radio: "The meteorological situation at twelve hundred hours. A vigorous depression centred over the Northwest will extend to all parts of the country..."

The priest stepped out of the side door of the chapel.

"Men," he said.

A sheepman with his cap tilted on the Kildare side of his head nodded respectfully. The others waited for the priest to drive off.

"He was asking me the other day how the farming was going?" said one of the sheepman to Nan and me, walking part of the road home with us. "I said to him, 'The farming, Father, is fuc ---- is finished,'" he amended, respectfully for my mother's benefit. "'The factories are giving the lowest prices ever.'" "'Our Lord, himself, the Lamb of God,' says his nibs, 'was sold for only thirty pieces of silver.'"

"'Father,' I said, 'if you had him at the mart on Tuesday you wouldn't get a bid on him.'"

TURF CUTTING RIGHTS

"I'm going to the mountain to cut turf," my father announced in the pub. The other drinkers roared laughing. Why would any man living in the coal-mining village of Arigna want to cut turf? The smell of turf smoke in the air might be a feature of rural life in the West of Ireland, but not in Arigna: in its place we had the thick smog and sulphur reek of native coal fires.

"Have you rights?" someone asked.

"Who's bothered any more about rights on the mountain?" my father said. "I'll cut turf on the first bank I come to."

A discussion started amongst the coal-miners about the great men going long ago, and the amount of turf they could save in one day; men who could blacken the mountain with turf. But that generation was dead and buried, and it was doubtful if there was even a proper turf cutting *sleán* left in the village? Might a garden spade or a hay knife be used instead to strip a turf bank? There was general agreement that cutting turf in neat level benches, or 'spits', was an art in itself. And you had to take into account the quality of the turf on different parts of the mountain. Sitting on high stools around the bar, the coal-miners saved so much turf in theory that the owner, Mick Flynn, finally said: "Someone open the back door or this turf will never dry."

*

After the dinner, a midday affair in our house, we tackled the ass and cart, the ass being more of an all-purpose vehicle for the mountain terrain than the grey Ferguson TVO tractor. We left the surfaced road and turned up the steep incline of the bog lane. A loud fart came from the ass when the strain came on the tackle: "He's switching over to the diesel tank," my father said.

After the green pasture fields, hedged around with brilliant yellow flowering gorse, we met rock and heather and drifts of lovely white bog cotton. A mountain hare ran a wide circle along the horizon, took a sideways leap onto a new course and making a fool out of our Sally, who returned panting, happy like us to be on the mountain more for the fun than any reward.

We were amazed when we spotted a neighbour preparing a turf-bank further on. Slipping away from the pub, he had rushed his dinner and reached the mountain ahead of us. He had his jacket off as he laid claim to the first turf-bank beside the bog lane. Two days later the place would be fenced off more securely than Fort Knox.

We continued as far as Noone's worked-out mineshaft, where the coal and slate coloured lane ended.

"*Go back…go back… go back,*" a disgruntled grouse squawked as it broke cover and flew from the turf-bank that we decided on. Unloading the tools and tea-making things, we then heeled-up the cart and tethered the ass on a long rope. My father lit a Woodbine, using the match to burn off the old heather. Smoke drifted towards the sky like a rebel uprising. When he finished his cigarette he cut the first layer of poor, wiggy turf. The second spit was better; good black turf that my father said would dry as hard as a goat's knee. He cut into the turf-bank in benches and each slice of the *sleán* scored the soapy black peat in a hound's-tooth pattern. I had the job of barrowing away the buttery new sods for scattering.

We were working for about an hour when Tommy Tivnan arrived in a spruce white shirt, a *sleán* across his shoulder, whistling "When I first said I loved only you, Maggie." He gave us a cheery wave and set to work on the opposite turf-bank.

Johnny Guihen was the next man to arrive. He was a coal-miner who grazed his cattle on the mountain for the summer between Rockhill pit at one end and Derrinavoggy pit at the other end. He counted his cattle in the morning and the evening on his walk to and from work and he pointed out to me the dangerous airshafts in-between, and warning me to keep clear.

When we got parched for tea, we found a forgotten clamp of turf and started a fire with twigs inside a ring of stones. We boiled water in a saucepan without a handle. Tommy Tivnan brought over his sandwiches. Tasting of turf-smoke, the tea was, as my father said, strong enough to trot a mouse on, but we ate with keen open-air appetites the soggy egg and tomato sandwiches seasoned with salt from a twist of newspaper. Then Bernie Gilhooley appeared, rolling up his sleeve and sticking his arm in the cold, mineral-dark waters of the bog hole to soothe the rheumatism caused by an old pit injury.

"Keep your head under for ten minutes, Bernie," said Johnny, "that'll cure all your aches and pains."

Sitting down drinking his tea, my father got a midge in his eye.

"As small as you are and as big as the mountain," he said, "and you had to fly into my eye."

We nearly burned as much turf as we saved while the yarns were told around the fire and heroes were remembered: Lester Piggott – "If he was only riding a donkey, bet on him." And Mohammed Ali - "Too bad, too fast and too beautiful."

My father tossed the dregs from his cup and said there would have to be further trips to the mountain to finish the cutting and the scattering; to foot or 'rickle' the turf into little pyramids, crowned with a level sod along the top to keep off the rain; to gather the turf in clamps and to build the clamps into bigger reeks; to haul the turf home in loads using the ass and cart, with more loud reports from the ass going downhill when the strain came on the breeching.

After only half-a-day's work, my arms, my legs and back ached and I felt daunted by the work that lay ahead. But I was young and would soon get my strength back.

My father, however, would have this cloudless summer on the mountain and then his lungs would progressively weaken - not from coal dust or silicosis, but from a lifetime of smoking; his movements gradually narrowing to gestures and finally a complete stop. He died sitting upright in his bed at home, missing the next breath of air.

But on that open day he sat hunkered before a turf-fire, happy to be sharing around cigarettes amongst men resolved to claim back an acre of mountain. Coal-miners with their best years over. Men whose work had kept them underground for so much of their lives, yet their faces raised now to catch the light and a sweet mountain breeze under a faultless blue sky where the larks sang their hearts out.

PRESIDENTIAL ARRANGEMENTS

The parish hall had a telephone installed and got renamed the Community Centre. Everyone still called it 'the hall', but the President of Ireland, Mary Robinson, agreed to do the formal re-opening, despite the handful of objectors who said they wanted nothing to do with, 'that Communist'.

Shortly before the official visit, Nan went to the post office to collect her widow's pension. As she gathered her few bits of shopping for the week she got talking to the other women. Widows mostly, like herself.

"Are ye all set for the big day?"

"We have nothing done."

"Oh."

"We're very short of hands."

"Is there anything I can do to help?"

"We need someone to do the flowers."

"For the President?" The blood left Nan's face. "I wouldn't like to tempt providence."

"You have a great pair of hands."

"I couldn't," she said. "Not the flowers."

"What's stopping you?"

Courage, she thought.

On the day of the Presidential election she had paced her kitchen all morning talking to herself. Finally she put on her coat, tied her headscarf under her chin and walked to the parish hall in the teeming rain to vote. In the privacy of the polling booth, with a pencil in her hand and nothing showing only her toes out under the partition, she voted against generations-deep family politics for the Labour Party presidential nominee, Mary Robinson.

Now, her hands started to shake as she settled her bill and fixed the clasp of her purse without taking in what she was doing. The other women kept pressing her to do the flowers and finally she said, "I suppose I could give them a shake and a shuffle."

*

There were times when she found it hard to forgive Matt for dying on her and leaving her alone. And when her twin sister Lil's husband, died a month after Matt, leaving both sisters without support, she sank lower than she had ever been in her life. She thought she was going to lose her mind. It got so bad there were times she thought the best for her would be to crawl into the grave and die.

She got sick, worse than the time she got every one of her teeth out. And the doctor who came to see her told her straight out the sickness would pass, but the decision to get well rested with her alone. Or as the doctor put it, "I can get you back on your feet but you have to pull up your socks."

She started to take an interest again and put her energy into her garden. Now under the stairs where poor Matt once tossed his working clothes, she had the comfort of lavender in bunches, trays of sand-dried roses, Chinese lantern and crisp dried bouquets of helichrysum in the fragrant dark.

On the day of the final preparations for the Presidential visit, she arrived with a load of dried flowers, a block of oasis, tying wire and her secateurs. She had a spare paintbrush too, along with the flowers, just in case the other women thought she might be looking for a soft job or getting above herself.

At the hall door, she met the priest. His black shirt was speckled with paint and his hands were freshly gloved in white weather-coat emulsion.

"Have you many helpers?" she asked.

"The few reliables," he said.

She put down the flowers and raised her paintbrush.

"When you don't have horses," she said, "you have to plough with asses."

"Are you any good with a paint roller?" the women asked as soon as she walked into the hall. "You can follow us, taking out the streaks."

"And don't let His Nibs water the paint."

190

After she had the women's toilet painted, Nan worked by herself on the back porch and the scullery, giving the wall over the sink a finishing coat for good measure.

The priest came in with the hair on his head wet. "The rain is landed," he said.

"It won't leave a bit of paint on the walls," Nan said.

"I'll say a prayer for a dry hour."

"As long as that breeze is blowing from the far mountain," said the man along with the priest, "you needn't bother your arse, Father."

At midday they stopped for a mug of sweet tea and shared around a homemade apple tart. After the break, one of the organisers took Nan aside. "We'll finish the painting. You start on the flowers."

On the table in the back room lay a stack of bouquets and donations of fresh flowers, along with extra bundles of ferns and greenery. She felt weak at the sight.

"I'm not sure I'm able," she said.

"Do what you can." The other women left her to get on with the job.

She soaked the oasis in water and set out the flowers in separate bunches while she concocted arrangements in her head. It took her a long time to get started, but once she got going the hours raced. When she had the arrangements for the stage done and the centrepiece for the podium finished, she put delphinium and dried roses in little china bowls to ornament the dining table.

The other women had started to come in and out of the room to set the table, arranging cruets, cream-jugs and place settings. "Lovely," they said to Nan when they looked at the flowers, "they really brighten the place." But there were too busy to give a considered opinion.

The priest stuck his head around the jamb of the door to see how everything was going.

"I suppose ordinary five-eights like us have no business here tomorrow when the President lands?" said one of the women. "It's only the big licks that will get to meet her."

"They're all calling now at the last minute," the priest said, "thinking the work is done and they'll get a handy job in the morning. But I'm not going to have this room full of people tripping over the President. Only the women that were here today will be on duty tomorrow."

*

The drum and fife band in the car park played a marching tune, but only a half-hearted clapping followed. People were afraid to lower the hand shading their eyes from the bright sunshine as they looked down the road for the first sight of the State car.

"She's not coming," one man said. "You'll see no President in this village as long as the hole in my backside is looking at the ground."

"She's here," the crowd shouted him down, and a round of applause started.

A black motorcar with two pennants on the front pulled up beside the shop with the pyramid of toilet rolls on display in the window. A clean-shaven uniformed man, the President's aide-de-camp, jumped out. He was followed by a skyscraper tall girl who carried a handbag big enough to hide a revolver. The aide-de-Camp opened the back door. Mary Robinson got out. Instead of her usual polo neck, she wore a silky, sea-green skirt and tunic and jacket that made her look even thinner than she appeared in the photographs.

"God love her," Nan said to the man standing at her shoulder. "There isn't a pick on her, no more than myself."

Her neighbour was a heavyweight man with a big head and a rosy complexion. He wet his lips and said: "I hear ye have a great spread left out for her, roast pheasant, tae and fish."

Without warning, a young boy with a hard, narrow head and a loose mouth broke away from the crowd and made a beeline for the President.

"That's a slap for you when you get home," his mother threatened from the sideline, but he followed the President every step of the way.

*

A couple of lads stood each side of the back door into the hall. One wore a baseball cap and the other had a knitted wool hat. "Steward", said the paper badges fixed on their jumpers with big safety pins. There was a strong smell of porter.

"Is Her Poloness here yet?"

"She's on her way," Nan said shortly.

"Go on in," they opened the door for her, and then reached back to drain the bottles of stout left on the window-ledge. There were more empty Guinness bottles dumped in the sink. "Good men, ye couldn't wait," Nan said under her breath, gathering up the empties to put them out of sight.

She found the other women in the back room where the President and the invited guests would eat. They were all dolled up, wearing new dresses, blouses and matching jackets and skirts. She wondered if her navy jacket and polka dot dress were good enough for the occasion. "It's neither suede nor leather," she said. "But I got it at the right price. I call it my recession outfit."

"It's lovely on you," the said, but they were good friends and even if she had one eye missing, they'd have tried to convince her she was better off and better looking without it.

Only one person would serve the President. The others were in charge of the food. Nan had to make the coffee. "The good news," they told Nan, "is that we have a percolator to make fresh coffee for the President. The bad news is you can't plug it in until the speeches have finished or you'll blow every fuse in the house. We're all morning saying Hail Marys over the fuse-box."

It was an old fashioned percolator like the one she had learned to use in England. She filled it with water and ground coffee from a packet, while the others carefully arranged brown bread and smoked salmon on bone china plates. A damp knife was used to divide a home-baked fruit flan and a springy sponge cake.

Someone said they should take a peep at what was happening. Nan didn't like to leave her post, as she was nervous enough already, but the other women led her away by the arm.

Climbing the wooden steps at the side of the stage, they found a place behind the curtains where they could watch the goings-on without being seen.

The President had entered the body of the hall to view the stands. She stood under the Irish Countrywomen's Association banner and looked at their hand-knits and quilt-work. She moved to the plaster-cast garden ornaments being made on an area allowance enterprise scheme. She inspected the stack of blue plastic trays loaded with mushrooms from the local growers. She nodded her head with keen interest while a young lad explained his school project: a design for a slurry spreader for small tractors. She asked another man if he had ever been encouraged to start up a small business?

"I did," he said.

"What happened?"

"It got smaller."

She moved on.

The young buck with the hard, narrow head never left the President's side. He stuck his head into every one of the official photographs. When the President bent down to examine an antique flat-iron, the young lad, his mouth open and the snot rattling in his nose, leaned in over her shoulder to view the exhibit along with her. Her aide-de-camp hadn't a look in.

The place was mobbed by the time the officials led the President to a padded seat at the front of the hall to view the entertainments. "We're going to start with a few slides from the musicians," the priest announced.

After the music, the children came on stage dressed in white shirts and shawls that hung down to their ankles. Their faces were painted and they had pikestaffs and white bands in their hats. More coloured ribbons hung from their sleeves. They said they were the Ribbonmen and launched into the song-and-dance-routine learned at school. Flash cameras popped as proud mothers snapped souvenir pictures. The oath-bound outlaws of the past - Rory of the Hills, the Peep-o-day boys, the Molly Maguires - all had become figures in a children's pantomime.

The official guests mounted the steps leading from the dance-floor to the stage. They were all men. No one except the tall girl, who seemed to be acting as a bodyguard to the President, even looked in the direction of Nan and the other women standing in the wings.

"Your Excellency, the President of Ireland, we welcome and thank you most sincerely…" The welcoming speeches dragged on until the man with the video camera recording the event had to ask his partner for more film.

"She'll be white in the head before they finish," Nan said.

"Sssshhhhh…" went the call from the front to the back of the hall when the President stood up.

"I was delighted to have the opportunity to be here today," the

President began with her chin in the air, her eyes directed at the ceiling, as if the words she was searching for were written on the rafters. "I am most impressed by your sense of community spirit, a spirit that is quite tangible here... And I have to turn to the children of this area, your singing, dancing and acting, *Go halaínn ar fád*... And I was delighted to meet *Mná Eireann*," she said, with her fingers pinched for emphasis as she plucked a loud cheer from the air and nodded her head. "To see the extraordinary skill of women in the home. The State has not always recognised her value, her status..."

"She's looking at your flowers." The other women prodded Nan in the ribs and she missed the next bit of the speech. Then it was over. The applause came in waves and went on for several minutes. "Wouldn't you think the television people would be here to film this," one of the women said.

"We were on the television twice," she was told. "Once when we were on strike for three months and once when the mines closed."

Nan looked at her watch and said: "We'd want to get our skates on." They made a dash for the tea-room.

The instructions from the President were to keep the dining area as private as possible; she would have coffee and nothing more. The local officials and committee members "would eat anything that was shoved into them."

When Nan plugged in the coffee percolator the lights dimmed. She bit her bottom lip. The electricity flickered but stayed on and the coffee began to simmer. With the grace of God and extra strong fuse wire the President got served. The meal passed off without a major disaster. Nan reckoned they were like a show-jumping team that rattled every fence on the course, but miraculously finished with a clear round.

She was washing the returned plates in the scullery when the tall girl came in and said the President was running late. To avoid delays the President would leave by the back door.

"Christ, it's a good job you gave this place a lick of paint," one of the women blurted to Nan just as the President walked in. Everyone froze. Nan wondered if she should curtsy first or dry her hands with the tea towel.

"I've put you to a lot of trouble," the President said.

No one spoke. The President looked at them in turn, smiled at Nan and said: "The hand that rocked the cradle rocked the system."

Her aide-de-camp appeared to say the car was ready. When no

one followed the President out of the scullery, Nan broke the silence. "Begod, we'd better see her off."

The lads on duty at the back door put down their porter bottles as the President passed and they waved in a group as the State car left the village.

The women were giddy after their face to face encounter with the President, and the lads looked sheepish when they were told: "The steward badges should have said Guinness. But ye might as well come in for a cup of tea. There's any amount of food left-over."

The crowd broke up quickly after the President left. The back room was cleared. In the hall, the stands were dismantled and the exhibits put away. The other women went home and the parish hall fell silent. Only Nan stayed behind to take the floral arrangements to the chapel. On her own for the first time that day she stood and looked out from the empty stage. Then she bowed and gathered up the flowers.

MUSEUM PIECE

Daly, Lavin, Reynolds, Keegan, Cull, McManus, Early, McDermot… Names from the coal-face. Pitmen. Gilrane, McPartland, Flynn, Dooley, Cullen, Rynn, Tivnan, Guihen, Gaffney… Generation upon generation. A three-hundred-strong father-and-son labour force, employed in the North Roscommon coalfields of Arigna.

A company coal lorry brought the coal-miners to and from work at the Rockhill, Derrinavoggy and Rover mines. More came on Honda 50 motorbikes. These 'hair-dryers on wheels' were often without signal lights or a headlight, sometimes even without brakes. One evening the white squad car stopped a Honda 50 with nothing on it, only the driver's brother. Both men raised their white eyeballs to the guard, their faces black with coal dust after a hard day working underground.

"Where are you coming from?" the guard asked.

"The bakery," the driver said.

*

Visitors to Arigna got a shock when they met these black-faced men on their way home. But coal-miners were cleaner than a lot of farmers; they had to have a bath every day. And the young lads with jobs in the mines always arrived at a dance spruced and gleaming with money aplenty in their pockets.

Working in the coal-mines, you learned to rely on the man using the coal-cutting machine or the pickaxe alongside you. At break-time the miners might stuff photos of topless women in the pit bag of a young fella, knowing his pious mother would find them when she was getting his lunch ready the next day. Or the man who brought his lunch to work in a biscuit tin found his lunchbox nailed to the floor. But teamwork got the job done and the mines generated a fierce closeness.

It was an easy thing to spot the Arigna crowd together at the same table on a Saturday night out. When a new priest in the valley remarked at a dance in the parish hall: "There are very bad acoustics in this hall," the pitman standing beside him bunched his fists and said: "I don't know who these acoustics are, but if they start any trouble here tonight, Father, they'll get the worst of it."

*

The coal-mines were tiny by the standard of most industrialised countries. The men often had to lie on their backs in water, using a handpick or a short-handled shovel to get at a thin seam of coal under a ledge of rock. It could be a three-mile walk to the coalface, followed by a day spent 'rooting like a dog and sweating like a pig'. You never saw a 'styme' of daylight from the time you went underground that morning until you surfaced again that evening. And when the clocks changed back to winter time, pitmen went to work in the dark, worked all day in the dark and came home in the dark.

They spoke an underground language of 'sumps' and 'gobs', 'peacetime', 'hutches' and 'clips', 'bings' of slate and 'bullets' of rock, 'caps' for detonating 'spats' of dynamite. They worked in teams: the miners working at the face cut coal alongside shovellers and drawers who took it out, and brushers who replaced the rock and slate to keep up the 'roof' after the coal was removed. They were overseen by the firesmen who gave the orders. Monday was their day off. Tuesdays were rough.

The pitmen were under no illusions about their choice of career. As one coal-miner said: "The work was hard and the pay was small, and no matter how little you did, you earned it all."

For most of their working lives the coal-miners in Arigna used carbide lamps. The rocks of carbide in the bottom chamber of these lamps released acetylene gas as the solids dissolved under the drop of water from the top chamber. Experienced pitmen had the control of these gas flames down to a fine art. A steady flame of light was vital. If you ran out of carbide underground you could end up stranded in total darkness. Men hid reserves of carbide in waterproof containers for emergency use, and when these private stashes got stolen they lit the darkness with curses.

At the pit entrance a red lamp burned night and day under a picture of the Sacred Heart. The coal-miners blessed themselves at this spot before they went underground. Strangers who visited the mines out of curiosity often found the experience of the mineshaft so frightening they never got 'past the picture'.

The coal in Arigna produced no explosive gas compared to English or Continental coal. But a job in the mines had its dangers. Falls of rock were a constant threat, and most of the time you worked alongside coal-cutting machinery in confined spaces in poor light. Every branch of every mine had its own noises and subterranean character, like a ward for the elderly at night. The sheet-rock shifted and the pillars propping up the weight overhead groaned and resettled. Water dripped. Voices echoed. The compressed air passed your face like a disembodied whisper. And beyond the glow of the lamps the darkness was complete. It took steady nerves not to keep looking over your shoulder, working alone and immured in these black vaults under the mountain.

The older pitmen talked of seeing lights underground down empty branches of the mine where no one had set foot for many years. Seeing strange lights was an augury of misfortune. A more real but invisible danger was the 'black damp'. If you stumbled into a pocket of bad air, or the reek of poisonous fumes left behind where a blast had been let off, then you understood what the old miners meant when they spoke about the black damp. The only warning sign was a flickering flame as the carbide lamp began to fail from the lack of oxygen. If your lamp went out, all you could do was run as fast as your legs could carry you, keeping your head down to avoid the bullets of rock jutting from the low roof and hope to God the air up ahead might be breathable.

In spite of the dangers, fatal accidents were few and far between. But if you worked too close to dynamite and got caught by the blast, the fragments of blue-black debris stayed in your skin a lifetime. After a deep cut the slate and coal dust stayed in the scar, like route marks on a map of your days underground.

The temperature in the mines stayed constant. A cavernous still air that made you sweat when you worked, yet the minute you stopped, you were perished to the bone.

"It's hot behind the wheel," said a lorry driver to a coal-miner one summer's day.

"It's hotter behind four wheels," said the pitman pushing a hutch loaded with coal back onto its rails.

There were feuds and disputes over the years and one prolonged and bitter strike that left the colliery workers without a wage over Christmas. But the real problem was the quality of the coal, which in real terms it wasn't worth what it cost to mine. The Arigna coal bought to supply the local power station at Lough Allen had to be heavily subsidised to compete with Welsh, English, Polish and American imports.

The coal reserves began to dwindle. The power-generating station at Lough Allen was at the end of its operating life. And the fate of the coal-mines was sealed. At a packed meeting in the parish hall the matter of the miners' redundancy payments was settled. The coal mines closed in 1990. The power station shut three years later.

*

Despite the closure the coal-mines maintained their curiosity value. And on a bank holiday weekend a poster with a miner working at the coal-face appeared, announcing Arigna Mining Display, a three-day exhibition of coal-mining artefacts, photographs and videos.

On a set of folding screens in the body of the hall, scores of snapshots donated by the community were on display: the pitmen at their trade, together with family and school photographs. It was shocking to realize how many of the miners were dead. And it felt as strange to be looking at hand-tools once commonly used by the miners now labelled and catalogued and displayed in glass fronted cabinets. To see what had been essential in your lifetime become a museum piece.

People as they went around the exhibits gradually fell silent, almost a chapel-going hush. The pick-axes, carbide lamps and the short-handled shovels, the implements of manual labour and coal-cutting machinery parts had an atmosphere, a power similar to holy relics. Nobody was calling the pitmen saints. But the torn caps and pit helmets were laid out like vestments, with old account books and colliery receipts for sacred manuscripts. And the large-scale, professional black and white photographs taken by Derek Spiers years before of the pitmen at their work, looked like industrial Stations of the Cross. Images that froze and distanced the coal-miners from their lives. Icons. With a litany of names to recite: McLoughlin, Lynch, Woods, Wynne, Moran, Conway...

CONEY ISLAND

In the first brittle days after I got married to Carmel, days of tender feelings and dislocation, days of changing values and perspectives, I went walking out to Coney Island. Out across the tidal sand-flats, the whole solitary day before me, to explore this unexpected turmoil in my heart.

What was I looking for? An outing across the strand at Sligo bay, or an act of passage to mark the new course my life had taken, away from Arigna, away from the home place.

I had one clear purpose: to write a colour piece commissioned for Saint Patrick's Day. My starting point would be Saint Patrick's wishing chair, a boulder deposited by glacier ice-floes or, if you preferred, a holy artefact brought there by the power of a saint, to the Northwest corner of Coney Island off the North West Coast.

Given my state of mind, I was hoping for cloud-shadows passing dramatically landward across the strand, sweeping changes of light on the surrounding mountains - Ben Bulben, Killogeboy, Sliabh daEain and the Lady's Bray. But Queen Maeve's tomb was shrouded in mist, Knocknarea a sullen, looming presence and the sea and the sky washed in a pallet of greys: seashell, oyster, and mother-of-pearl.

An avenue of 14 stone pillars posted the straight, safe path, sunk in salt-water, the strand a reflection of the sky. In my mind the journey outwards was spiced with danger, though my table of the tides said different. And soon the water became speckled with the sand sprouted by countless lugworms as the sound continued to empty. Sea birds pursued the retreating water-margin, curlew calls and a flight of sandpipers lead the march onwards to Coney Island.

A single two-storey ruin with red-roofed outhouses stood against the skyline. A flock of gulls descended on inland pasture and ploughland. Instead of the sea I got the smell of the cowherd, descendants of the cattle once walked off the island at night, when the sight of the deep water in the channel would not frighten them. And walked all night to the markets and fair days of Sligo and Leitrim: Ballisodare, Colloney and Manorhamilton.

Ignoring the direct route I took the long way round the island. In every sandy hollow I spotted ghetto-dense warrens terraced with rabbit burrows. Coney Island: Rabbit Island. Hound of the brake, orange stain behind the ears, tail an immaculate white, ears alert to my footfall, ducking away by the dozen. The same rabbit colony that had provided meat for the pot while their pelts were sold to make fur trim for gloves during the War years.

A baritone ocean broke along the coast at Strandhill, a fallen chapel visible on the headland at Killnaspugbrone. This was the site where the saint was said to have camped before his visit to Coney Island, praying to be delivered from the magic wiles of blacksmiths, druids and women.

I watched the cormorants out on the rocks where the seaweed lay in a broad iodine bandage. For a mainlander the sea here had a regenerative smell: a medicinal salt aroma and the full spume and splash of the open Atlantic. The next parish being America, 3,000 miles west, and another Coney Island named after this one, the story goes, by a homesick sailor from Rosses Point. Separate islands but partners too, like the matched flights of sea birds skimming the breakers.

The day was mild, but the sea roared. Even in the sheltered coves there was a big valve radio hiss of sand and foam and backwash. Then gunshots. A heavy bombardment. The cannon peal and crack of surf behind the rise.

On Carty's Strand the sense of isolation was fierce. Here tradition allowed the island men to marry only women from the mainland, so the girls just grew up and left. Now the place was furnished only with emptiness, such emptiness, and frazzled ends of rope.

Next the guardian lighthouse on the Black Rock peeped over the rim of the island and rose steadily from the sea. And there it was. A boulder in the soggy ground, made magical by legend. Saint Patrick's wishing chair: a seat, a footrest, a cradle for one elbow, its high back upholstered with moss and lichen. Behind the stone seat the well had returned to nature, the damp mud cow-tracked, the eye of the well closed with watercress.

At this storm-bitten corner of the island the treeless fields gave way to the line of breakwater rock. The sea plunged in thundering folds that went deep under the island, the vibrations magnified beyond all proportion to the size of the waves, their echoes booming and rolling back out across the channel.

One wish only could be granted each year to whoever sat in the saint's chair. But to rest in that seat was to find myself centred in the profoundest calm. And what more could I wish for: so deep in love, on the brink of the sea, as close now as I would ever be to the big eternals.

THE GLASS WOMAN

PART THREE

VII

The hospital loomed: a multi-storey glass-and-brick edifice all function and no frills. Uniformed attendants in vans with flashing yellow beacons policed the car parks for revenue. Ambulances slouched heavily along the curved driveway, inbound and outbound from Accident & Emergency. Taxis halted at the set-down area as the maimed on crutches with legs in plaster-casts, arms in slings, heads bandaged, eyes patched, were ferried to and from the main entrance.

Outside the entrance the smokers stood under a canopy finding no shelter from the building's cold turbulence. Inside the main door a woman crying sat on a bench. Glancing into the emergency area my mother spotted 'a fine young fella' knocked out cold on a trolley. We passed the accounts desk, ignoring the flower stall and the shop, to go directly to orthopaedics. My mother baulked at the elevator saying she and her sister Lil suffered from claustrophobia.

We took the stairs though we had several flights to climb. My mother was surprisingly nimble on the stairs: one benefit of walking the mountain roads practically every day of her life. But even as I admired her sprightly pace I felt sorry her, as she must have known her twin sister Lil was on the brink of the last confined space, and we were at the start of a death-bed vigil.

We trooped along the shiny corridors, passing signs for Male Surgical, Female Surgical, Intensive Care, Coronary Care and Maternity: life going out of the world and life coming into the world and the majority battling to hold on.

Finding the right ward, we spotted Lil laid low in her bed. She had her eyes closed. She was resting. Her sisters, Teresa and Kathleen, had been in earlier to see her. No doubt Lil had done her best to talk to, even entertain them with the little strength she had left. We were supposed to arrive in one group but our visit got delayed. It had taken me all morning to persuade my mother to come to the hospital now rather than wait – to use my mother's phrase – 'until Lil settled in'.

As we approached the bed my mother whispered, "Such a thing to have to face. Poor Lil."

Lil's feeble appearance pierced me right through. One nightmare after another had struck this courageous woman with pulverising speed and callousness: a breast removed three years ago, temporary remission and then osteoporosis symptoms that turned out to be cancer in the back bone. And just when she had won back a little ground the thing she dreaded most: to fall and end up with broken bones in an orthopaedic ward, knowing that, in all likelihood she would never see home again.

Lil raised her head.

"It's just us," my mother said meekly.

Lil's left arm was strapped up in a sling and she had a clear plastic oxygen mask over her mouth. We could hear the hiss of the gas in the tubing. The doctors were trying to stop a lung infection developing into pneumonia.

"How are you today, Lil? You're breathing sounds better." I said.

"If I live to get over this," she said.

As she moved up in the bed slightly, we urged her to leave the mask in place. With that oxygen mask over her mouth and her arm in a sling, I suddenly saw her as a brave little boat alone on a raging sea, the waves at any moment threatening to swamp her and all the time she was moving farther out of sight, headed for an unknown horizon. But by God she hadn't capsized yet.

She told us about the people who had been in to see her; the neighbours and relations and the women who picked mushrooms along with her, including her employers.

"People are very good," my mother said.

Considering the trauma she had been through, I was amazed how calmly Lil spoke and how readily she accepted this dreadful setback.

"Were you talking to Sean?" she asked.

"The windows upstairs are going in today," my mother said. "He's holding the fort to make sure the job gets done right."

"And then there's the hay to finish before the weather breaks," Lil said. "How well everything had to come together."

Her anxieties had shifted from her physical pain and discomfort and now clustered around expressions of worry about her son and all he had to do around the house and on the farm without her.

I glanced at the chart on the clipboard at the foot of the bed. It meant practically nothing to me except the up-and-down course of the blood pressure and temperature readings and the letters PRN - *Pro Re Nata* - prescribe as required and beside the acronym the brand of tranquillizer.

A nurse arrived with a cordless telephone, saying there was a call for Lil. The caller turned out to be her daughter Geraldine. She had already come home to see everything possible was being done for her mother, and had returned to America only days before Lil had her fall. Now Geraldine rang her mother every day to talk and to get an update from the care staff.

Wanting to give Lil some privacy, I moved off to speak to the woman in the opposite bed. She told me she had been admitted with broken bones in her foot after falling down the stairs at home. She laughed all the time as she recounted her accident, how her foot was driving her mad, it was so itchy under the plaster-cast. Then nodding in the direction of Lil, she said, "That poor woman is a bag of nerves." Though she laughed as she said this, her remark brought home to me that Lil was very frightened.

I noticed Lil gesturing to me and I returned to her bedside. Glancing across at the woman opposite, Lil said, "That one never stops laughing. She was laughing when she told me she broke her foot, but I couldn't see the fun in falling over."

Lil might be frightened and sedated but she missed nothing going on around her.

"Geraldine is still on the line," Lil said and she handed me the phone. "I asked her to have a word with you."

Backing away from Lil's bed towards the corridor, I steadied myself to hear bad news all the way from America. But Geraldine said that no tumour had been found nor any sign of cancer detected in the hipbone. Her mother had cracked her hipbone as a result of the fall and it was a clean break. An orthopaedic team was treating her for the cracked hip and a further injury to her shoulder. Her next appointment with her oncology consultant was over a month away. After that she spoke about strategies to help her mother once she got out of the hospital and was back at home. I was too surprised, and uncertain of my facts, to know what to say. The call finished and I handed the phone back to the nurses at their station.

I felt totally confused.

Lil had advanced cancer of the spine. Admittedly, the tests done to identify additional cancers had produced only question marks. But Lil was so weak and underweight the doctors had ruled out more rigorous testing. The evidence of my eyes told me Lil did not have long to live. It was a shocking and even callous thought, especially in a building where the cut-and-thrust of daily business opposed injury, sickness and death. But how much could this woman be expected to endure?

Maybe I was being too pessimistic. Whenever Carmel and I went walking on a fine day, I was the one on the lookout for rainclouds. I believed danger did not go away just by refusing to think about it. But in Lil's case I was, perhaps, too despondent. Lil had surprised us once by making it home. Her children were the only ones privy to Lil's true medical condition. And if her daughters were looking at care plans for a time when Lil would be allowed home again from the hospital and her son was fixing up the house to make it comfortable for his mother to pass the winter, they must have grounds for being so positive.

Before I got the chance to work out the ramifications, a piercing electronic noise broke out in the corridor. One of the hospital porters arrived to tell us we had to leave the building. There was a fire drill in progress.

"We'd better go now," my mother said to Lil. "We're neither useful nor ornamental here."

"See you again," I said, taking Lil's hand and promising we would be back shortly. The alarms were deafening but there was not a trace of urgency. Visitors drifted nonchalantly from the ward while the patients sat tight. The only person to show surprise was the nurse who stopped in her tracks and stared at my mother. Thinking it was her twin sister Lil with her handbag and coat on - making a miraculous escape.

VIII

Amongst her sisters Teresa was the most forceful and headstrong, her assertiveness heightened further from working most of her life in the postal service in America. She had her mind set on giving Lil the initial, month-long course of injections of the 714X therapy she'd found through the Internet.

"We gotta start these injections," she said.

"It's not that straightforward," I replied.

We had gathered for lunch in the basement restaurant of the hospital, Teresa and myself, my mother and Aunt Kathleen. Around us the visitors mingled amongst the doctors and nurses; the visitors anxiously trying to find some place to settle, while the medical staff slumped in chairs looking run off their feet.

"If we wanted to give Lil a herbal drink or a tablet nobody would take any notice," I said. "Even if the care staff disapproved of the medicine, Lil could take it when the doctors weren't looking. But with the best will in the world, a qualified doctor or a nurse who injected a patient with an unsanctioned medicine could end up struck off the register."

"Then we'll do it ourselves," Teresa said.

"I've looked at the video that came with the treatment," I said. "It takes half an hour or more for the procedure. And Lil would have to be taken out of the hospital and brought somewhere to give her the injections. Supposing something went wrong with no proper medical supervision. What would happen if Lil got worse while she was away from the hospital? Or if she died soon after an injection? There would have to be an inquest. Somebody would have to explain the needle marks. Somebody would have to take responsibility. And her children might have something to say about that."

Teresa looked to my mother and Kathleen for support but nobody spoke.

"So that's it," Teresa said. "We do nothing?"

Teresa wanted to do what was best for Lil. But that greater good was at the nub of our dilemma. All of us wanted what was best for Lil, only we couldn't agree on the right course of action.

Teresa had her hopes in the treatment, an American belief that whatever the problem, this too can be fixed. My mother was too close to Lil to be making critical decisions. And Kathleen was down-to-earth but keen to keep the peace. Meanwhile her daughters were out of the country, Geraldine in America and Maeve in England. Both were professional women with better lives abroad than they had ever been able to find in Ireland before leaving this country during the miserable and murky 1980s. It upset Lil that she did not have her daughters living nearer home at this time, but it would likely upset her even more if both women walked out of positions that hard work and determination had brought them to spend months around her bedside, prodding her with needles.

The youngest in the family, Sean, had remained at home to work on the land and to mind his mother. Over the years, he had kept Lil company in that fiercely remote farmhouse. But faced with the loss of his mother, his shield against anguish and grief was to stay close to the farm and keep everything running as normal as possible.

Uppermost in my mind was the detrimental impact the poking and prodding with needles would have on Lil. But I had a phobia about needles, and my thinking might be clouded. In addition, my faith in pharmaceutical conglomerates was limited. Neither was I an outright advocate of complementary medicine. When I got sick I went to the doctor, found out what was wrong with me and took the prescribed medicine. In most cases I felt better.

However, complementary medicine was now an established feature of everyday life: acupuncture, homeopathy, reflexology, body massage, faith-healing sessions, bio-energy therapy, reiki, herbal tinctures and yoga, craniosacral therapy, shiatsu and aromatherapy. It is human nature to seek alternative remedies - the wealthy because they could afford them, and the poor because they can't afford proper treatment in the first place. And desperation is a powerful money earner so much so that a massive money-making industry is now cherry-picking both ancient and modern health treatments that can be bought off the shelf of any health shop in Ireland. The world-wide web is also awash in new treatments and the latest cancer drugs. Some of the drugs are in development, some await approval from the relevant licensing authority, while others are strictly on the fringes of orthodox medicine or beyond. But with credit card and mail order you can select from a world of treatments to be dispatched and delivered to your front door. Which highlights a fundamental principle of the Internet: information is useless without discernment.

Following the family conference in the restaurant that day, where the difficulties I had raised practically put the kibosh on the injection therapy, I set about finding help. Two days later I was in touch with a woman with her own complementary health clinic who said she was ready to consider the injection therapy. I called around to meet her in person and to give her the background material. She could look the entire package over to form her own opinion of the situation and the treatment.

Her clinic was in a side room of a lovely quiet house in the country. I immediately liked the feeling there. And she made an equally good impression. She was calm, perceptive and warm. She smoked. A human failing that appealed to me.

"If you felt you could give these injections we'd employ your services," I said, speaking on behalf of the family.

We talked for an hour. She asked for more background information. When I mentioned Lil's earlier breast cancer procedure she said different emotional manifestations were associated with each of the breasts. Finally she said she would accept the job, on condition that the family met with her to discuss the nature of the undertaking and to give their informed consent. Her response was everything I had hoped for.

When I rang Teresa with the news she was overjoyed.

But we could not proceed with the treatment until Lil was stronger and could be moved in and out of the hospital for the half-hour alternative treatment sessions. In the meantime, Lil rigorously followed her own strategy: eating as much as possible to keep up her strength while avoiding any mention of the cancer besieging her now featherweight body.

We visited as often as we could. Increasingly I felt our lives becoming unmoored, adrift and rudderless in the wake of Lil's illness. In the hospital the staff followed their rosters, knowing the work they had to do, knowing when their individual shifts started and finished. But for the visitor, time unravels in a hospital. The heat made me thirsty and heavy-eyed. Stodgy snacks and meals eaten on the hoof built up in the stomach, with no proper exercise beyond walking the artificially lit corridors and stairs. And where the patient was gravely ill even a talkative family like ours found conversation a strain.

Lil's condition improved and declined in a seesaw rhythm that saw ground gained in one domain while lost in another. The steroids that reduced the swelling in Lil's ankles made her face bloated. The powerful antibiotics that fought her pneumonia allowed the cancer to waste her body further.

When it was clear that Lil was steadily losing ground, Aunt Teresa again tackled the orthopaedic team about the injections. They said it was a matter for the cancer specialists. But Teresa kept pleading with the medical team to read the material on the chemical composition and purpose of the 714X medication.

"Please don't get annoyed with the doctors," I said. "They're doing the best they can."

"I guess you can draw more flies with honey than vinegar," said Teresa.

After being stonewalled for a fortnight, she finally persuaded a member of the staff to take away a copy of the technical information on 714X to consider its merits.

Teresa thought this concession a real breakthrough. But I was sceptical. Would the medical profession respond seriously to a member of the public equipped with information taken directly off the Internet? Standing close to the private area where the staff gathered, and unashamedly listening for their reaction to the material from Teresa, I heard a voice say, "More X-files."

It was hard to blame them. And Lil herself got around the problem by agreeing when she spoke to Teresa that the injections were a good idea, and similarly agreeing with her doctor when he ruled out the treatment at this juncture.

Calling in one evening with my wife Carmel, we spotted my brother Dermot and Lil's son Sean. They were standing by Lil's bed on the point of leaving. We stood a respectful distance back at the entrance to the public ward, while Sean said farewell to his mother, ending on the promise of 'when you are better.'

On his way out Sean noticed us. We nodded hello. He looked badly shaken and he kept walking, headed for the elevators.

"They're moving her to the Hospice," Dermot said.

"What did you say to Lil?" I asked.

"We said the hospital needed her bed for emergency cases. She was going to the Hospice to convalesce."

Dermot went after Sean while we went ahead into the public ward. It was the middle of the week and two of the beds previously occupied were empty.

"I'm being moved to the hostel," Lil said. "To convalesce."

"That's right," I said.

In the course of our chat that night she said the word 'hostel' several more times. I got the impression she wanted to trip us up. She wanted to make us correct her. She wanted us to say she was being moved to the Hospice. And if she was being moved to the Hospice she was a goner.

Every time Lil mispronounced it, I noticed the flicker in her eye, as if calculating whether some way could be found to reverse the inevitable conclusion embodied in the word. Again she spoke about going to the hostel. She even called it the hostage. Then she corrected herself.

"Hostage! What am I saying? I'm not a hostage."

IX

Word came that Lil had taken a turn for the worse. The family were sent for as a gale swept in from the Atlantic. The wind tore the leaves from the trees. Storm water sluiced through the gutters. It was hard to find a space at the hospice and I parked the car some distance up the road, walking back towards the hospice with my coat collar turned up and my head cast down. Around me the gale shook the streetlights, rattled the metal road signs and piped an eerie lament on the upright poles.

There was a tradition that said when a member of the Beirne family died the banshee cried. The gale-force gusts whipping around the high buildings, the air full of leaves blown in shawls and the noise of those poles acting as wind instruments in the dark made a perfect urban banshee.

Visiting hours were over and I had to press the buzzer and wait for a member of staff to admit me to the building. While I stood there the chaplin drove up and sprang from his car. When the nurse opened the door I allowed him to hurry through ahead of me. In the corridor I stood aside as a second nurse rushed into a sitting room carrying a tray loaded with teacups and plates of biscuits. Another nurse holding the teapot followed her. The tea was for the family of the person who had just died. The first of three cancer deaths in one night.

Maeve stepped out of the private room which the hospice had generously allowed her mother. She had arrived in time to talk to her mother, she said. Soon afterwards Lil slipped into the coma. Her younger sister Geraldine's flight from New York had been delayed. But when Geraldine spoke to her mother to say she had arrived at her bedside, Lil opened her eyes and squeezed her daughter's hand. The acknowledgement given, Lil closed her eyes, done with holding out.

When I walked in the family were present in the room. The atmosphere was calm. I stood by Lil for a time and then moved aside to be with my mother.

Later, I spoke to my sister-in-law Josephine. She said Lil had been great, talking directly about how she had conducted her life and her legacy to her family. Her last words to the doctor who had been so kind to her during her stay in the hospice were, "God leave you your health." To her family she said she was prepared for death, naming the things she wanted done and the things she wanted right. She asked for her bill in the local shop to be settled.

Until the last, Lil's instinct was to do the decent thing. But it was only when I heard how important it was to Lil to settle her account that the bind of anger and desolation in me at the pain suffered in life by those who least deserve it came apart. Death broke her back. Not life. In life she was unbowed. And I knew then I would mourn Lil, but I would not mourn her lot. Just as Lil never bemoaned her lot, knowing where her priorities rested, good humoured, clear-eyed and assured right to the end.

*

In the funeral home they sat in a line along the far wall: Lil's sisters Nan, Kathleen, Teresa and her brother Bernie Joe, together with Lil's daughters Geraldine and Maeve and her son Sean. The crowd of mourners outside filed in one by one to pay their last respects to the dead woman and the family in mourning. Each signed the book of condolences. Each paused at the open coffin. Each stood to say a prayer, offer a gesture and brush the hands or forehead of the corpse with a fleeting touch.

Meeting the mourners took over an hour. People kept coming forward; people from the locality, people who had travelled, people who felt it important to be there, people greatly moved by the loss.

"If only she knew the value people had on her," my mother said, reeling from the size of the turn-out.

The Rosary was recited and the responses given.

Then the mourners went outside while the family made their private gestures of parting before the closing of the coffin. The closing of the coffin was hard. It was our last ever sight of what death had left of the woman we knew. And the tense, pent-up grief became more acute watching the undertaker locate the lid on the coffin and give a final twist to the fasteners finished in the form of a cross.

It was cold outside the funeral home where the mourners stood about talking in the shade. "I never stood outside a funeral home yet but I wasn't perished," a voice said. And when somebody wondered why so many funeral homes were built in such cold spots, they were told: "It's the undertakers drumming up more business."

Many of the mourners were, in fact, elderly and susceptible to the cold. An ageing community of widows and bachelors, small farmers, coal-miners and sheepmen, neighbours and relations turning out to mourn the loss of a good neighbour and good woman. The population turning out in force to see off one of their own.

The largest crowd generally came to the evening removal when the remains went from the funeral home to the church. But the following day at the funeral service the crowd was just as large.

The funeral bell tolled and again the family sat in line, this time in the front seat of the church nearest the coffin. After the prayers and a thoughtful homily the coffin was shouldered and seen out with incense and sobs on the shoulders of the men in dark suits. Before the cortège started for the graveyard, and the final committal to the earth, people came forward to talk to the family outside the front porch of the church.

They knew my mother was the nearest one to Lil, and many approached her to share a comforting word and clasp her hand.

When it was over my mother showed me the purple welt on her right hand. It was sore and badly bruised from shaking hands - shaking the arthritic hands of old neighbours, the solitary hands of widows, the soft hands of the young and the desk-bound; the broad hands of pitmen with coal-dust marked scars, the precise hands of shopkeepers and mushroom pickers, the hands of labourers and farmers disfigured at the joints with the scars and weals of a lifetime's hard work, the hands of country people that never realised their strength.

X

I was working at my desk just days after Lil died when the call came to turn on the television. By the time I learned what had happened one of the World Trade Twin Towers had gone, it's South Tower already an after-image. Replays of the passenger jets wilfully flying into the two skyscrapers, one following minutes after the other were constantly repeated. But I couldn't look away. Black smoke billowed from the remaining North Tower of the World Trade Centre, while before my eyes, and the eyes of the television-viewing world, people who had gone to work that morning like any other morning were faced with the choice to jump to their deaths or be burned alive. Then the North Tower collapsed. Despite the knowledge of the lives that must be lost in the falling rubble the first impression was stunned disbelief at the sight of something so majestic toppled.

Later I heard from a friend an account of what was missing from the television coverage. The noise. In the aftershock of seeing each tower crumble from the skyline onlookers were struck by a monstrous sound. They described it as a discordant rumble unlike any sound in nature, as if the gates of an infernal dimension opened to leave all who heard those catastrophic tremors forever shaken. And I could not help imagining that for one instant in the wake of that otherworldly noise there must have been a silence. A silence not unlike what the dispossessed native Indians once called the Great Silence: the silence of going into limitless mystery alone

From childhood my imagination had been saturated with American TV and Hollywood images. And I recognised an iconography I cherished in this attack - but utterly perverted to bring about such an emblematic mode of carnage.

All transatlantic passenger fleets had been grounded and neither my mother's sister Teresa nor her brother Bernie Joe could fly home after Lil's funeral. In the kitchen at home we listened to the news for the latest updates. Everybody sat tight, discussing the situation over endless cups of tea by the stove.

Teresa said it was the fault of Bill Clinton. His cutbacks had left the US navy with no ships, the army with no weapons. America was a soft target. When he was in power he ran the defence forces into the ground and spent the money on health.

219

"Blessed are the peacemakers," my mother said. "And I'd sooner see money spent on health than missiles."

Attention moved to the rescue effort at Ground Zero and the attempts elsewhere at getting back to normal life. A week later, Bernie Joe got a flight to Chicago where his family had been waiting anxiously. The following day Teresa was able to fly home via John F Kennedy airport. It was a strange but fitting farewell with all of Ireland shut down for the national day of mourning.

Here, we mourned with feeling. But if the Irish took a day off work the Americans kept going. Whatever about the citizens of Manhattan, the American people appeared to be more determined than reflective on the complexities that launched these hijacked passenger jets flying with such deadly purpose out of a blind spot.

In the days after the attack on America, and in the aftermath of Lil's death, I kept noticing symmetries. The double one figure of September 11: identical elements standing side by side with unforgettable force. The sensation of what was no longer there still vivid and present in the mind. The mingled impressions of a visit to the public viewing gallery of the World Trade Centre and a memory of Lil sitting in her kitchen and looking out her window towards the lane: the contrasting scales but equal consequence of the worlds beyond those respective panes of glass. Lil telling me she was like a 'glass woman', and the brittle impermanence of the Twin Towers as they shattered like they were made of glass. Time after time I was brought up short by these parallels. In a discussion of the terrorist attacks on America, one commentator remarked that there had been threats before but the American people had escaped. Until September 11th when America ran out of luck. Like Lil, who had said to me, "I thought I might get away without this." And finally, the loss. The irredeemable loss of life.

Closer to home, I asked my mother how was Lil's son Sean getting on since his mother died.

"Poor Devil," she said. "He'll find it lonesome."

Yet she was the one who had lost a sister. And my mother admitted how lonesome she felt without Lil. Especially when the hours dragged on a quiet Sunday around the home place. Then she wanted to pick up the phone and call Lil. Only her twin was not there anymore. The sister towers and the towering sister. Gone.

THE SPIRIT WIND

THE SUMMER WIND

I took the "Galley Bridge" over the Shannon River with Lough Allen and Sliabh Anierinn on the right. On my left I could see Arigna and the home place. Ten tall white wind turbines soared above the heather crest of Kilronan Mountain. The sunlight struck the spinning blades like prongs of lightning. The spindles of a second wind farm stood out against the sky further north over Corrie Mountain.

Some people hated the sight of these 'windmills'. I had no problem with them. They looked as playful as whirligigs on a breezy day. Beautiful in their strange isolation, they took the lonesome look off the mountain. Plastic and new, massive and sleek, their purpose was to claw energy from fresh air. Turbines built on a mountain under a sealed honeycomb of mine shafts: a complex of silent and unvisited tunnels from which the mineral energy had been depleted. Minus their ballast of coal and human labour force, the mountains appeared ready to take flight. Ready to wing away on these massive propellers.

Is that what made me stop to consider the sight, the sense of absolute absence these windmills inspired? Built to capture invisible energy from an invisible element, their scale and polish lacked human reference. Living men once sweated and hacked, scraping their bare knuckles as they tunnelled for coal beneath these mountains. There had to be fossil fuel, heat and smoke and steam pressure to deliver power to the national grid.

But that was not the full picture.

Despite the closure of the mines, the coal sales-yards on the site

221

of the early iron foundry and the narrow-gauge railway siding in Arigna were bigger and busier than ever in the history of the valley. The first, experimental 'bagging plant' had evolved over the years and now mass-produced low smoke and smokeless fuels to accommodate a more environmentally sensitive market. Imported coal dust and starch-binding agents were used today in place of the native coal in a largely automated process of fuel manufacture, sales and distribution managed by Arigna Fuels. As I passed through the valley the cooling chimney was going full steam and a fleet of lorries rolled between the stockpiled fuel and the industrial buildings where my brother Terry worked for a new generation of the Layden family.

Out of curiosity I passed the sycamore tree at the entrance to the home place and took a spin up to the wind farm.

The turbines on their tall stems were not fenced off yet. I got out of the car and positioned myself directly under the first towering white turbine, trying to step inside an elusive experience. As I craned my neck beneath the guillotine drop and rise of the giant propeller blades I began to feel dizzy. A memory stirred - of wisps in flight as a whirlwind raced towards our meadow field on the farm on the mountain years ago. A fairy rush of wind, headed our way, the leaves of the hawthorn hedge swishing strenuously while all around stood calm. A spout of air entered the hayfield, making a dervish dance of dry hay and lofting a spiral of chaff and straw into the air while my brothers and I chased the spirit wind.

SAVING FACE

The meadows had been cut and the hay allowed to rest in swards while the threat of rain passed over the country. We turned the swards on Thursday afternoon with another low front skirting the west coast. We turned them again the following day to toast in broken sunshine, the high pressure holding up. Now the hay lay ruffled and exposed, a crop open to ruin but not yet fit to be harvested.

To season hay you need a light breeze and full sunshine. Six fine days will make quality square bales. Six good days of summer, not much to ask, unless you lived with an island climate where it was most changeable, on a 'disadvantaged' mountain farm in the northwest of Ireland.

Here the climate was an obsession. Every conversation opened with a remark about the weather: "Fine day, thank God," was answered with, "It's a short stay." "Soft day," met with "As long as it doesn't get any softer."

Predictions were generally pessimistic, like my grandmother who remarked during one of the finest spells of weather on record: "We'll pay for it yet."

World events and regional news went unheeded when the hay-saving began. We fine-tuned our attention to the radio for the midday forecast and the long-range farming forecast on Sundays, where the presenters split hairs between a slight improvement and remaining unsettled.

Predicting a dry spell was too important to be left to satellites, computer-generated weather simulations or radar reports from the coastal stations. When filaments of white cloud laced the heavens in 'mare's tails', 'goat's hair' or a 'mackerel sky' each oracle display was read for the threat of rain; if birds flew inland and the trees looked silver – the undersides of their leaves turned back by a strong breeze, a storm was on the way; when the midges were mad the pressure was falling; when the swallows skimmed the fields and the daisies closed their petals the rain was close at hand; when you could see the far mountain clearly it was going to rain; when you couldn't see the far mountain it already was.

In such circumstances, the decision to cut the meadows might appear to be a calculated gamble. You measured the odds, rolled the dice and accepted the outcome. But that never happened in practice. Once the haymaking started a transformation swept over the home place. Melodrama and madness took hold. Personalities changed overnight. Even the most easy-going farmer got overtaken by the nearest thing to the warrior Cuchullain's warp spasm, swinging his tractor through the gap into the hayfield like the *gae bolga*, with the set of a man who meant business.

A few who owned small, inaccessible hill fields continued to build the traditional haycocks or trams. After a succession of wet summers there had been a switch to silage crops cut by a harvester and compressed into mounds in the farmyard before being covered with plastic and weighted down with worn car tyres. The newest method was silage wrapped in black plastic bales, known in these parts as 'black babies'.

For some reason understood only by themselves, the crows loved the colour black. And crows arrived in flocks, ripped open the plastic and spoiled the bales. Farmers had to paint their bales another colour for protection. They splashed aboriginal patterns, zig-zags, spirals and stripes and on the bales with white emulsion and a broad brush, spelling out obscene messages with one letter to a bale - CROWSAREBASTARDS was a famous example. The result was an unintentional but vigorous new rural art form.

There was another, more timeless, art in the colours of the individual farms. In high summer this countryside looked beautiful. The newly cropped fields shone flaxen and gold, the fields cut early for silage gave the deepest green, and every shade between moss, lime and apple was painted into this living patchwork by the timing of the harvest and by the distribution of pasture, meadow and fallow land. Nationwide activity that foddered both livestock for the winter and the coffee-table-top photography-book industry of Ireland.

At this time of year farming territory extended beyond farm boundaries to the public roads. Twin trails of mud announced a gap and the path of machinery crossing. A sharp bend in the road could be blocked by an enormous tractor with terrifying spiked machinery hooked to the back like mediaeval instruments of torture. Motorists, tourists and delivery vans must wait to overtake while the farmer made slow but unyielding headway. Mechanization was the thing. No one anymore wanted to get down off the tractor.

Progress had been swift since the old man stood to watch his neighbour spread manure on the meadows using a donkey and what appeared to be a set of traditional creels. But these creels were a new invention, known in Mayo as a *purtóg* and known locally as the Yankee Tipper. Made of iron, the bottoms of both creels were hinged so that pulling a lever the farmer could simultaneously release their loads. The old man scratched his chin in admiration at this breakthrough in farm technology and said: "By God, they'll not improve on that."

Like my two brothers, I lived away from home. We were married now with other jobs and other lives. But when the forecast was good and the meadows were knocked, a call went out and all hands returned for the hay saving. It was an imposition, an encroachment on married lives and careers, but we spread the burden between us.

My mother could not be persuaded to retire. Farming was not her livelihood: it was her life. "What would I be doing sitting in the house all day?" she said as she walked the meadows to inspect the state of the hay.

She had kept her head above water on this small farm through good years and bad. She had made countless sacrifices to educate her three sons away from her world and everything she cherished. At different times it looked like one or other of us would return to take over the farm. But it was my mother who said: "It's a form of abuse to leave a child a small farm in the west of Ireland."

We made square bales each year, which involved a heavy share of manual work. This year I had company; a volunteer who was born and reared in the country like myself, but who worked in an office job. Even though he was on holiday he yearned to be involved in the summer work. The hay harvest had become for both of us a fusion of strenuous leisure activity and meaningful work.

While the hay dried we went looking for a man with a baler. We caught up with him in a neighbour's field, greeted the men working there with a wave and stopped the tractor. We were heroes when we returned, having secured a booking.

A shake of the wild hay rattle plant and the crisp scrape of the seeds inside the cut flower head told my mother the hay was in perfect condition.

"It's cracking," she said.

We were so close. All we needed was a baler before the evening dew, before the rain. The sound of the wind set our nerves on edge and we kept a close eye on the dark clouds gathering at the butt of the hill. We dared not imagine there had been a breakdown and the baler wouldn't make it.

Then we heard it. The baler had entered the field, to pound and bind the crop into neat parcels with the rasping thud of an iron lung, keeping our hopes alive.

Our hands were soft so we used gloves to collect up the bales that tumbled from the chute. For the first hour we sweated out the Rioja wine drank over a late dinner the night before. Fizzy drinks arrived and were passed around. And we remembered other cures for the thirst: the gallon from the spring well, buttermilk and water, 'bull's Milk' made by steeping grains of oats overnight in a gallon of spring water, the bottle of 'Fun' red lemonade bottled locally by a company called Drino, or the Tinker's can used to carry to the field hot tea already coloured with milk.

All of us remembered the work, the rituals, the enjoyable parts of working in the meadow, but we could not be classified as farmers. We did not have the relentless craving for land, livestock and "dry money" that signified the true farmer. We were not the sort of men who considered a visit to the cattle mart each week, to wallop a bullock along the broad of its back with a cattle-stick while shouting "Don't be making a pet out of him", a treat as good as a sunshine holiday. We had no talent for recognising the early symptoms of that catalogue of animal diseases and their treatments aired on mid-evening radio. We did not follow so keenly the Brussels bureaucracy: the schemes, subsidies, quotas and levies to be collected, dodged, abused or manipulated so as to come in with a profit at the end of the farm year. We were not as quick with an answer as our neighbour who when ordered by a visiting inspector to disclose how much land he owned in Leitrim said: "I have grass for two, and water for thousands."

The trend towards large-scale, homogenised European farming methods was far removed from our earthy, early experience. An unsentimental willingness to do whatever was required had always been a necessary part of managing a farm. But the pressure to rationalise was taking farm management into a territory where part-timers no longer belonged. A territory with a new language: of production strategies to hold down the reproduction overheads while increasing the reproductive output. Or pushing animals to their biological limits to synthesize food tissue. Or portion preparation regimes in which animals are designed from the embryo to the plate: an acceptance of livestock as reproductive mechanisms, with all the horrors that attended this treatment of living creatures as industrial units.

There was another grim fact to be considered: if you are compelled to make a living from 23 acres of mountain land, farming became a form of enslavement. Your name might be on the deeds of a small farm, but you never owned poor land, poor land owned you. And this form of hardship had produced its sorry share of rural bachelors and skinflints. Like the farmer who was too mean to buy a hot dinner for himself on a fair day. Buying a packet of dillisk from a stall instead, he shoved it and his change into the top pocket of his jacket and nibbled the seaweed while walking his bicycle home in the dark. Only to find when he got home that he'd eaten the fiver in his pocket along with the dillisk.

"Bullocks, briars and bachelors, that's all you'll find around here," my mother once remarked. And as the rural population continued to fall, the trend had been to blanket-cover poorer farms with conifer woods, a biological monoculture, devoid of nature or interest. Fast growing plantations, fashioned for tax relief and investment portfolios, now surrounded the roofless gables of the original homesteads. The better-quality fields near the roads were sold for sites for new bungalows for a rural population now largely employed within urban service industries.

A trickle of outsiders always came to the area looking for a cheap place to live. Continentals had arrived in the late 1970s and early 1980s in such numbers that a local musician on tour in Bavaria sent home a postcard saying he found that country very like Leitrim: the place was full of Germans.

To the population of local farmers, the Europeans who bought farms were picture straighteners. They imposed order on the flooded, rushy fields and the overgrown hedgerows. They dynamited the rocks dug deep drains, fertilized every square inch of ground, putting up plastic tunnels and massive barns painted Federal green. As one farmer said after a visit to a model farm owned by a couple from Holland: "If you had a bit of shite behind your ear they'd plant it with tulips."

When the money spent on improvements ran out, the new arrivals ran out soon after. They discovered a simple truth: a farm of land in the west of Ireland was a wonderful asset if you didn't have to rely on it for a living.

In the 1980s we also had the Crusties, an unfair but descriptive term for the self-styled New Age travellers. Many were English and had come here to escape either urban crime, drugs, squats, broken homes or the career plans of their parents. Their trademark nose-rings, shaved heads and pony tails, waxed-cotton coats, in-your-face attitude and a body odour that would stagger a horse meant they were not always popular additions to the community. At one music gig a crustie with the inevitable dog on a string approached the doorman.

"Is it all right if the dog comes in?" he asked.

"Sure," said the doorman. "The dog can come in, but you can fuck off."

Yet as one old farmer surrounded by conifer plantations remarked about the encampment of New Age arrivals in the neighbouring wood: "They'll talk to you anyway. More than the trees will."

The early 1990s saw a remarkable influx of new people and returnees to the area, due in part to a nationwide economic upturn. The cause of our more local resurgence was a canal, a freshwater navigation system that connected the River Shannon in the South of Ireland to the Erne waterway in the North. In a visionary act of reclamation the Shannon-Erne waterway was renovated with automated locks and bridges with sufficient clearance, not just for canal barges, but for motorised family-sized cabin cruisers. A silted artery unclogged, it brought new life and vigour to a previously numb and paralysed region.

The process of cultural cross-pollination was a good thing overall, and it was encouraging to find an organic garden and plant nursery won back from wilderness, an oak-wood tree planting project, the colourful window frames on an old restored cottage, its garden crowded with flowers and someone indoors trying to get the hang of a tune on the fiddle. But life on a small farm continued to teach its same hard lesson: back-breaking labour for dreamers and romantics.

*

We gathered our freshly made square bales of hay into stacks spaced evenly about the field. The bales would lose half their weight in moisture if we could leave them out overnight. But no one liked the look of the clouds at the butt of the hill. We loaded the bales on the prongs of a cocklifter linked to the antique grey Ferguson diesel-20 tractor, stacking 12, 18 and sometimes 20 bales at a time. The steering went soft, the tractor reared up and I had to sit on the bonnet to get the front wheels back on the ground.

Our muscles ached, our eyes itched and our fingers were sore. But the first few drops of rain were as good as three extra men in the hayfield. In one concentrated push we finished the harvest, a chore that used to occupy the entire summer. "A quare change," someone remarked, compared with those bygone days when the hay had to be cut with scythes, and the twin sounds of the corncrake and the rub of emery stones sharpening steel blades could be heard all summer.

When the bales were safely gathered in the barn we walked home exhausted through the stubble of the cleared fields, sharing a tremendous sense of accomplishment and elation. Even though we had been using machinery all day, this was a moment of pure wonder, a falling into step with nature and the timeless rhythms of the countryside: the opening of the human heart to the potent force of the harvest.

At home, we sat on the garden wall. Nan had the kitchen table set for a meat tea, with cooked ham and homemade soda bread, lettuce, tomatoes and fresh scallions from her garden. While we waited for the kettle to boil, we swigged bottled beer and shared yarns after the day's work.

The onset of the rain inspired a story about a crowd caught drinking after hours in a local pub. It was a wild, wet night and the door was shut tight. The guards had to force the door open and they caught the crowd inside red-handed. But the late-night drinkers said they were only delighted to see the guards. The rain had swelled the jambs of the door and they were waiting hours for somebody to rescue them.

The friend tells us about the veterinary student called to help out during the Foot and Mouth emergency. With her she brought a textbook, and she had the page turned down at the part dealing precautions against the spread of Foot and Mouth disease. Handwritten in the margin was a lecture note: "If Foot and Mouth is discovered, take off your clothes and comfort the farmer."

One yarn led to another. The pressure was off. We had been in the public eye for the last five days and cleared the meadows before the rain. If the rain had come sooner, and rooted the hay into the ground, it would not have been just a matter of a ruined crop. In this part of the country, if you lost the hay your judgement was open to question. You had made a conspicuous mistake in full view of the neighbours, suffered a devastating loss, and there was speculation that perhaps your poor judgment could go beyond lost hay.

After the supper we said our goodbyes and went our separate ways. Nan was happy. With the animal fodder secured, the farm would endure for another winter. Time kept changing the machinery and the methods of farming, but as it was in the beginning, is now and ever shall be, life on the land continues to be a struggle with unseasonable weather, rates of growth, animal health and the fickle demands of the market. The farm, like the meadow field, remains an arena, a gamble, a test of strength and skill, and a matter of luck and judgement after all the forecasts.

SCENT OF CREATION

Before I go, I take a walk in the twilight. Heavy drapes of perfume hang in the lane: the smell of honeysuckle at night. Wild woodbine. A fragrance so sensual, so evocative, the night air is clotted with this perfume. It enfolds the senses, this nectar of Salome, this concentrated smell of summer longing; a reminder of the torment of being a teenager, yet still too young to be let out to the dances.

I am alert again to that collaboration between memory and the sense of smell. This imprinting of the brain with odours, scents and traces, each implicated with a strong emotion.

A whiff of printer's ink so fresh it smudges across the pages of the evening paper and I am transported to a first summer job in the city. I've just shared a goodnight kiss with a girl I've met and I'm higher than the world, passing between terraced houses that smell of cabbage stalks and greyhounds chained in back allotments. And walking further again, to clear my head in suburbs wafting lilac, laburnum and lawn-cuttings, I reach the iodine-fresh sea at Dollymount Strand.

The copper-and-acid smell of old coins in my pocket is another familiar scent, warmed to the temperature of my father's hand, and seasoned with the loose shreds of tobacco that were always at the bottom of his pockets. And something more exotic: aniseed, from those buttery, black liquorice sweets he shared with me while chatting about his life in England. Telling me how his friend Ted Slater took him on a hunt to see how the huntsmen left a trail for the hounds to follow by using a rag soaked in aniseed. A snatch of small talk between a father and son the day he taught me how to shoulder, aim, brace, fire and take responsibility for his shotgun.

These are just some of the minuscule items in the endless back catalogue of scents and odours steeped in associations. Particular perfumes that ignite a nerve ending, press a retrieval button in the brain, and I don't just remember - I am right back there in a world I had thought beyond the reach of memory. However briefly, time pivots and lost experiences return with all their öriginal intensity.

When I sniff the faint ammonia smell from the gaps in the flagstone floor of the cow barn it is winter again and I am ten years old. Looking out into a farmyard covered in snow, I see sprinklings of straw and hayseed on the ground. Brilliant white sunlight bounces off the sparkling snow. It has taken a while for my eyes to adjust to the dark inside the barn, but now I see the dry fodder left in bundles at the cow-stakes with the animals chomping and rattling their neck chains. A moment steeped in mystery and pride, seeing these cattle in our care safely through the hardships of winter.

Whole ranges of childhood experience return with the smell of broken wax crayons found in the pocket of a plastic school bag while rummaging in an outhouse. And there are impressions too of my grandfather, Henry Joe, mending a harness with the cobbler's thread he called 'wax-end' revived instantly by the smell of pitchblende and leather.

And what about the household smells so loaded with significance: tea leaves stewing in the pot on the hob of the black coal-burning No 8 Stanley Range in the kitchen, soda bread baking in the oven, a hot iron on cotton sheets fresh off the wash line. Potent smells of domestic security and warmth. And their opposite. The atmosphere of empty rooms. Damp mould behind wallpaper. Coffin lining and casket brass. The smell of the clay from freshly opened earth, the perfume of lilies so redolent of farewell.

Over and above these loaded traces is the powerful musk of love. The faint and precious scent a mother finds between the wisps of hair on a baby's head. Travel and arrival smells. The scent of new territory and lost territory. The scent of creation and its opposite, the smell of everything passing. Aromas that cut to the quick of memory. Wondrous links between fragrance and recollection and deep feeling. The opening of the senses to that fragrant membrane in which we catch the breath of life.

NO MEADOWS IN MANHATTAN

At midnight local time on the island of Java I rang my mother in Ireland and got no answer. It was January 3rd, 2003, and Carmel and I were staying with her sister, Catherine, husband Sherif and their kids Eamon and Nadia in palatial, company-approved accommodation at Jl Benda 90, in the ex-pat enclave of Kemang in Jakarta.

Working as a teacher and an engineer respectively, Catherine and Sherif were college educated and prepared to pursue careers in their chosen professions, even if it meant straddling the globe in four-year postings at a stretch in Cairo, Abu Dhabi, Texas, Paris, and now Indonesia.

We had celebrated the New Year in Bali, and been treated to one of the most exotic and memorable holiday experiences of our lives, even though the Irish Government had warned its passport holders against visiting Bali on account of the terrorist bombs that exploded in the tourist district of Kuta on October 12, killing 202 people and leaving another 240 injured.

Bali without tourists is like Lourdes without pilgrims. Unthinkable. And the Balinese themselves had conducted all the necessary cleansing and appeasement rituals that their faith required, and could not understand why the Australians and the Americans especially were staying away or keeping out of sight in secure high-end tourist compounds. So when we got there we found the restaurant district in Sanur where we were staying dark and customerless with only a handful of places able to afford to stay open.

The safest spot to get fresh food was on the beach. And in the evenings we ate the catch of the day from the boats hauled onto the strand in semi-darkness under the tropical stars in the light and smoke of cocoanut husk fires. It was like going back in time before the advent of mass tourism. But we had also fallen off the radar where the rest of the world was concerned.

That my mother had been trying to get in touch while we were travelling was a concern. She didn't make even local calls lightly, and international calls were a rarity. But if the news had been truly urgent then more frantic efforts would have been made to get hold of us. And it was about mid-morning Irish time on Sunday when I finally got through to the home place.

"Bad news here," my mother said straight away. "Teresa is dead."

She could mean only one Teresa. Teresa in America. Her sister. The indomitable, forceful, health-conscious, generous-hearted older sister Teresa. The uncontested head of the family that everyone looked up to.

Teresa had died on Christmas Eve in her bed after she'd finished wrapping her presents. For Christmas Day she meant to travel to Connecticut with her daughter Maureen, husband John Willers and their daughter Erin, to celebrate Christmas in Connecticut with her son Brian, his wife Terry and daughter Katie. It was Maureen who found her Mom. Still in bed. Dead from massive heart failure.

My mother, who'd lost her twin sister Lil a year before said, "I was sure I'd be the next one to fall off my perch."

Instead it was Teresa who had not only passed away quietly in her sleep; she'd already been laid to rest. Dismayed and helpless I asked if anyone from our side of the family had been able to travel to America for the funeral.

Flights were impossible to book, my mother said. My brother Terry and his wife Josephine had found only one company on the internet offering seats. But they would accept only a sterling credit card transaction. Aer Lingus wanted an unaffordable €7,000 for the round trip.

Only Teresa's sister Kathleen stood a chance. Her daughter-in-law Niamh worked as a flight attendant. After a great deal of heroic wrangling on Niamh's part, Kathleen was told she should take hand luggage only, wait for word at the airport, and be prepared to be disappointed.

At the very last minute Kathleen said, "They told me 'run'. And they let me on the plane as they were closing the door. They found me a little seat in the cockpit where I sat with my legs dangling, and I could hear the captain and co-pilot, who were lovely to me, being told by the control tower to 'move up Shamrock Heavy' – the code word that we were clear for takeoff."

"And so by the skin of my teeth," Kathleen said, "I made it to the funeral."

In the 1960s Kathleen and her husband Pat Tuite had lived in Great Neck on Long Island as near neighbours of Teresa who'd settled on South 10th Street in New Hyde Park. Kathleen felt particularly indebted to her older sister because it was Teresa, she said, "Who first took me out to America, bonded me, and sent me to school where I learned to type."

Teresa and Kathleen's mother had earlier been to America in the 1920s. She'd worked as a housemaid for a Jewish family and then she got a job in a candy store and ice cream parlour in Manhattan on East 23rd Street. The business was owned by Scottish relations called Doonan, and the ice cream parlour was really just a front for selling bootleg gin and beer during Prohibition. Teresa's mother was the sweet young colleen, fresh from the old country, who served the children candies while old Doonan out the back filled the lidded quart cans that the children carried with beer to bring home to their parents.

After Prohibition the place became quite a fine bar which the Doonans sold when they retired.

Though she had several relations in Manhattan and Rockaway, Teresa's mother decided not to settle down in New York. Instead she came home with a massive trunk that I remember from my childhood taking up space on the landing in the home place. She'd filled the trunk with good coats and dresses, and returned with a war-chest to buy land and a dowry to get married.

By the 1950s, having reared her family on what she saw as a social status-giving twenty-three acre farm of land on the side of the mountain in Crosshill, her oldest daughter Teresa was old enough to book passage to America.

From the moment Teresa got established on the far side of the Atlantic she encouraged Kathleen to join her in the US, helping her sister to get a job that Kathleen said she really enjoyed, working for General Motors in Manhattan. "'Twas a great place to work," Kathleen said. "We even had shares."

Teresa also gave a helping hand to her youngest brother Bernie Joe. When he arrived in New York she helped put him through evening trades classes in Queens College, where he qualified as an electrician and got himself into a union, eventually finishing up in Chicago.

By the late 1970s Kathleen and Pat had decided to move back to

Ireland, having bought a small grocery shop in Celtic Park near Beaumont in Dublin. When they took on a larger supermarket in Kells, Bernie Joe and his wife Mary also came back and took over the shop in Celtic Park.

They wanted their children to be educated in Ireland. But when the kids were reared Bernie Joe and Mary returned to live in Chicago. His electrician's union background allowed him into the trade again where he got a job in the McCormick Centre, helping to mount and dismantle the lighting set-ups for massive trade expositions. At the start of 2000 the secretaries, he said, had pressed placards to their office windows saying '20°c in Here'; while on special rates for working in the sub-zero conditions outside, Bernie Joe and his buddies happily raised their own sign saying '$50 an Hour out Here'.

Bernie Joe also said that up until 2002 they'd used pagers on the job in the McCormick Centre. And he'd just gotten a new cell phone in December, when the very first call he got was to tell him that his sister Teresa was dead.

Teresa alone had stayed the course in America. And where Bernie Joe and Kathleen were concerned, she was the uncontested head honcho in the family. The Omni-Momma who had looked after everyone. To the extent that Teresa had sent a portion of her wages back to Ireland every time she got paid to help her parents meet the cost of building the new two-storey farmhouse that became the home place that stands there today.

"And mise too," Kathleen confided. "Out of every pay check I earned back then I sent a certain amount on. I was single at the time. But Teresa was married."

As far as Teresa was concerned, however, anyone making a genuine effort – including her parents – could rely on her to put her shoulder to the wheel. This in turn meant that if she judged you a slacker she 'didn't leave a tooth in it,' as Kathleen said. She had no problem calling you a 'lazy bum' and 'a useless hoor' straight to your face.

Nobody who fell short of her standards was safe from her disapproval. So that one time when she ran to the local store to buy cold cuts and bread rolls for unexpected callers to South 10th Street, and then found that the bread rolls were rock hard, the next time she stopped by she told the store owner, "If I'd had the time, I'd have come back here and hopped them off your head."

After that the owner always told his staff, "Please see to it that the lady gets fresh bread".

It was the same in the 1970s when her mother broke her hip. "The rest of us," Kathleen said, "were humming and hawing about what was best. But it was Teresa who took the bull by the horns and contacted a medical man she knew in Dublin who ruled that their mother's heart was strong enough to undergo surgery. She had a hip replacement operation done and got a new lease of life, even making a trip after that to America."

Like so many Irish Americans with a strong work ethic, Teresa was unapologetically right wing and Republican. Values that she passed on to her children who'll happily put a spin on the old joke that Amtrak is a Native American word for late, and tell you that as far as they are concerned "Obama is a Swahili word for taxes."

Teresa never forgot that to get her start in life she had to pay to serve an apprenticeship and learn a trade with the Benson family who owned the village post office in Ballyfarnon. An industrious youngster, the only time Teresa ever got into trouble was when she and a bunch of her teenage friends went out onto the ice on the frozen Lough Skean outside the village. They had walked a good distance out onto the frozen lake when they heard loud cracking sounds underfoot. Teresa had the presence of mind to tell everyone to spread out but hold hands as they tiptoed safely ashore.

Her sponsors, who'd been entrusted to keep an eye on her, got such a fright they were tempted to let Teresa go, only they kept her on because she'd learned her lesson about walking on thin ice and never slipped up the same way again.

The apprenticeship she served in Ireland gave Teresa the means to apply for a job with the postal service when she landed in America. And she was still working in accounts, with a view to retirement on maximum benefits, when she died.

Back in 2000, Teresa had needed a triple heart by-pass. Even then, when the surgeon broke the news she fought tooth and nail with him to delay the procedure and put her on medication instead. But when she learned that she wasn't a suitable candidate, the very next time the surgeon made his rounds she asked, "When's my operation?"

"Oh so now you're in a hurry," he said.

She was strong willed and accustomed to getting her way. And yet she was a shy girl who never owned a bathing suit. She'd visit the beach, but only in a summer frock and high heels.

She had bright eyes and her mother's fair complexion, and she'd dated a couple of lads from home. Then in America there was a young man by the name of Walsh that she dropped after seeing what she called, 'The hump on him on a barstool'. Instead she met and married Pat Donnelly.

Their social life revolved around dinner dances given by the Armagh and Roscommon peoples' associations: long-table, linen and silver-service occasions where Pat looked the all-American male with his combed-back dark hair, sharp suits and cufflinks; and Teresa beamed happy amazement beside him.

In the early days, though, they lived in a small apartment that came with Pat's job caretaking the property for its owner. When it came to meeting the tenants' lists of demands they were under strict instructions to 'only give what you have to'.

The experience toughened up Teresa.

Pat, for his part, was more easy-going. He loved his football, his beer and a good yarn. And if he had worked for a while as a building superintendent he also went back to school and qualified as a refrigeration and heating engineer.

For their honeymoon Teresa and Pat travelled by passenger ship to Ireland. This was before the home place got built, and Teresa and Pat stayed in the original three-roomed, fieldstone built cottage where Teresa was born, with its big centre room and two bedrooms off that, one at either end of the house.

Living under the same roof at the time were Teresa's father Henry Joe and her mother Mary. Teresa's grandfather was widowed at this point and he also lived in this homestead in which he'd reared his family. Added to that, you had the twins, Lil and Nan, Teresa's younger sister Kathleen, plus the only boy and the youngest in the family, Bernie Joe. On his married sister's arrival Bernie Joe did precisely what we did when we were young and American visitors showed up: he ran off and hid in the hayshed out of shyness.

Pat Donnelly enjoyed his stay in Crosshill. On the first morning he took his razor and mirror outside to shave in the sunlight, only to see the hens run away with the soap.

Later, when Teresa's mother made him take hold of the handle of the dash to churn butter, as was the custom with everyone who called on churning day, Pat not only put on a big apron he stuffed towels down the front to dress up and act the part of the dairymaid.

He also borrowed Henry Joe's precious bicycle to cycle into a cattle fair in the town of Drumshanbo. Later that same evening, he was spotted staggering home in the company of his wife's relation, Billy Keegan. Both men were crooked drunk, and the busted front wheel off Henry Joe's bike was in Pat's hand with the frame hung around his neck to carry it up the short rise called the Lamb's brae. (Years later Pat's son Brian would also borrow Henry Joe's bicycle to head off with my brother Terry, and make a habit out of returning with the broken chain draped over his shoulder.)

Pat and Teresa made regular trips back to Ireland: to Pat's people in Armagh and to Teresa's home place. But it was the early visits especially that Pat relished, such as the time he found the teenage Bernie Joe building a road on the mountain on what was called an Emergency Employment Scheme.

Bernie Joe was labouring alongside Martin Reynolds and Tom McPadden – older men who wouldn't have a great reputation as strenuous workers. And when the foreman opened up the 'gang-box' with the tools in it they found it held only crowbars.

"What are we supposed to do with these?" Bernie Joe asked.

"They're for leaning on until the shovels show up," said Martin.

Pat loved such stories, especially when Bernie Joe added that the same Martin Reynolds finally had to quit the Emergency Employment Scheme after he got a rash under his armpit from leaning on his shovel.

Pat himself would have loved to retire to Ireland to run a farm of land. But if he ever tried being a farmer, Kathleen and Bernie Joe both agreed, he'd have starved.

Instead, Teresa and Pat bought a house in St. Petersburg in Florida where they intended to retire. Over the years Kathleen, Lil and Nan, and Bernie Joe all visited 'St. Pete's'. And my mother was there the time – before the 9/11 attacks – when Teresa flew down from New York to Tampa with a big tray of lasagne on her lap that she'd made to feed her guests. Then the plane hit turbulence.

Before either of them could retire to Florida however Pat Donnelly developed cancer and died, and Teresa decided that without Pat she might as well keep on working.

She still went to Florida, though she found it a lonely and

burdensome journey; to the extent that she once set out after a wedding in New York and drove the whole way to Florida with nobody to share the driving. She did the entire journey without stopping overnight.

Admittedly she said she'd never try that stunt again, having no memory whatsoever of the last part of the trip across the vast Howard Frankland Bridge that joins Tampa and St. Petersburg.

It was a phenomenal feat of endurance, especially as Teresa had her sister Lil in the car along with her, a woman who suffered the agonies of a junkie going cold turkey if she couldn't top up with hourly cups of hot tea.

Nan too when she travelled to Florida by car with Teresa made it her business to bring her own box of teabags and order a cup of hot water in the places where they stopped. Otherwise the servers were inclined to bring tall iced glasses of cold tea flavoured with mint.

After the death of my father, my mother thought about relocating to Florida for the climate and to be near Teresa. But she realised she'd never get used to a society where she witnessed an airport security man hurry on an elderly woman trying to find her passport, saying, "Keep moving, Lady." Whereas in Ireland when a senior citizen stood searching her coat and cardigan pockets for the passport she'd misplaced, the man at the Immigration desk said, "You have it well hidden, anyway."

The most heartfelt connection in any case was to the house and farm in Crosshill; a link maintained by Teresa and Uncle Pat and their two kids - our American cousins Brian and Maureen – over numerous crossings of the Atlantic.

True, when the American's rolled up at our door yet again, hefting their mountainous suitcases, their stay put my mother under ferocious pressure to find beds and bedding, to get in extra groceries, and above all to supply enough hot water.

There was no immersion, just the back boiler heated by the coal burning range, which meant that Nan had to keep the fire in the kitchen revved up on hot summer days. Even when she got the temperature up high enough, the heavy demand caused airlocks as the level in the copper cylinder dropped, or else the big tank fed from the spring well ran low. A quick cat-lick was all the rest of the household had time for as the Americans spent hours at a stretch in the bathroom, finally emerging from thick wafts of steam, the women dazzlingly made-up, and the men clean shaven and cologne fresh with a 'ruckus' of Irish banknotes in their wallets aching to be spent.

These holidays usually coincided with the hay saving. And Pat Donnelly loved to take up a pitchfork or a hay rake in his hand and join us in the meadows, even though the work he did was often undone in a flash as we dared our cousins to jump over the newly built haycocks.

Yet my father still found the time to take our cousins fishing with simple hazel poles and lines; expeditions to the river that they remember now as grown ups with their own families. And any sacrifices we had to make were more than compensated for by getting our hands on our cousins' Polaroid camera and portable cassette recorder.

As for the adults, they knew how to party. Late into the night you'd hear their laughter and the music of the accordion left behind from Bernie Joe's days in the parish drum and fife band, while his father Henry Joe took his old fiddle down out of the rafters.

Once again, as the Americans came 'home on holiday', we found ourselves on holiday in our own home. Then when Teresa and Pat took off from Shannon airport to return to the lives they'd made for themselves in America we had to go back to our own workaday existence.

Though not quite.

Because Aunt Teresa and Pat Donnelly and Brian and Maureen's visits changed us: our tastes were broadened and our understanding, respect and fondness sweetened towards this side of the family and their particular brand of American effusiveness and exoticism. These generous to fault relations who lived so far apart from us, yet through these family gatherings in the home place over so many delightful, sunlit summers brought to our lives such an unexpected and unquantifiable enrichment.

ACKNOWLEDGMENTS

"People are very good," my mother says in the course of this book. And I remember my mother with deep love and thanks for giving me so much. Thanks also to my whole family, my relations and my neighbours, the people of Arigna and the Beirne family in particular. I would especially like to thank my wife Carmel for her love, support, and belief in me. I am grateful to Nuala O Faolain for her permission to use an excerpt from an Irish Times Magazine article as an epigraph. Thanks also to Barry Lopez and his publishers. Thanks to Niall Kerrigan for the beautiful cover and to Danielle Kerins for her editing and publishing support of this reissue. Excerpt from About This Life published by the Harvill Press, 1999 © Barry Hulston Lopez, 1998. Reproduced by permission of the Harvill Press. .

While all of the work has been revised for publication, The Home Place contains a number of previously published or broadcast pieces. 'A Photographer Shows Up', was broadcast on BBC Radio 4. Versions of 'The First Garden', 'The Gift of Luck', 'The Money Changers', 'Opens Lines to Nora', Turf Cutting Rights' 'Museum Piece', as 'Names from the Coalface' and 'Scent of Creation' were broadcast on Sunday Miscellany RTE Radio One. Compact versions of 'July 1969', 'Legging It', 'The Perpetual Motion Man', 'Tom Swift and the Amazing A.I. Man' and 'Future Directions' were broadcast on Lyric FM in the Quiet Corner. 'Turf Cutting Rights' and 'The First Garden' were published in the Sunday Miscellany Collection edited by Marie Heaney (Townhouse 2000) 'The Wearing of the Green' (under the title Political Influence) and 'Famine Walls and Ribbon Codes,' were published in Force 10. 'Ploughing Season' appeared in Ireland of the Welcomes. Saving Face started out as a paper (A Long Way from the Leather Hinge) delivered to the Merriman Summer School and broadcast on RTE Radio One.

ABOUT THE AUTHOR

Brian Leyden's other work includes the documentaries *No Meadows in Manhattan, Even the Walls Were Sweatin'* and *The Closing of the Gaiety Cinema in Carrick-on-Shannon* for RTE Radio 1. He has written extensively about his native area for *Sunday Miscellany*. A popular reader he has been a guest of The Green Ink Festival, (London), Ireland and its Diaspora Writers and Musicians Tour of Germany, The Dublin Writers Festival, Flat Lake (Monaghan) and the Newport Festival Rhode Island. He is the author of the novel *Death and Plenty* and the short story collection *Departures*. In July 2009 he was awarded a Norman Mailer Writers Colony scholarship to Provincetown, Cape Cod. His libretto for the short opera *Humpty Dumpty* by Ian Wilson premiered at the Lancaster International Concert Series at Lancaster University, England in 2010. And with director Johnny Gogan he co-wrote the 2013 feature film *"Black Ice"*.

28424935R00154

Made in the USA
Charleston, SC
12 April 2014